the long and the short of it

the long and the short of it

he best-ever noodle and rice
cookbook with over 75 recipes

emma lee

southwater

This edition is published by Southwater

Southwater is an imprint of Anness Publishing Ltd
Hermes House, 88–89 Blackfriars Road, London SE1 8HA
tel. 020 7401 2077; fax 020 7633 9499
www.southwaterbooks.com; info@anness.com

Published in the USA by Southwater, Anness Publishing Inc.,
27 West 20th Street, New York, NY 10011;
fax 212 807 6813

This edition distributed in the UK by The Manning
Partnership Ltd, 6 The Old Dairy, Melcombe Road,
Bath BA2 3LR; tel. 01225 478 444; fax 01225 478 440;
sales@manning-partnership.co.uk

This edition distributed in the USA by National Book
Network, 4720 Boston Way, Lanham, MD 20706;
tel. 301 459 3366; fax 301 459 1705; www.nbnbooks.com

This edition distributed in Canada by General Publishing,
895 Don Mills Road, 400–402 Park Centre, Toronto,
Ontario M3C 1W3; tel. 416 445 3333; fax 416 445 5991;
www.genpub.com

This edition distributed in Australia by Pan Macmillan
Australia, Level 18, St Martins Tower, 31 Market St, Sydney,
NSW 2000; tel. 1300 135 113; fax 1300 135 103;
email customer.service@macmillan.com.au

This edition distributed in New Zealand by The Five Mile
Press (NZ) Ltd, PO Box 33–1071 Takapuna, Unit
11/101–111 Diana Drive, Glenfield, Auckland 10; tel. (09)
444 4144; fax (09) 444 4518; fivemilenz@clear.net.nz

Publisher: Joanna Lorenz
Project Editors: Sarah Ainley and Emma Clegg
Designers: Patrick McLeavey, Jo Brewer & Partners
and Ian Sandom
Illustrator: Anna Koska
Photographers: Karl Adamson, Edward Allwright, Steve Baxter,
James Duncan, Michelle Garrett, Amanda Heywood and
Thomas Odulate
Recipes: Carla Capalbo, Kit Chan, Jacqueline Clarke, Joanna
Farrow, Rafi Fernandez, Shirley Gill, Shehzad Husain,
Christine Ingram, Soheila Kimberley, Ruby Le Bois, Liz Trigg,
Laura Washburn and Steven Wheeler
Production Controller: Wendy Lawson

Previously published as *Rice and Noodles*

10 9 8 7 6 5 4 3 2 1

NOTES
For all recipes, quantities are given in both metric and imperial
measures and, where appropriate, measures are also given in
standard cups and spoons. Follow one set, but not a mixture,
because they are not interchangeable.
Standard spoon and cup measures are level.
1 tsp = 5ml, 1 tbsp = 15ml, 1 cup = 250ml/8fl oz
Australian standard tablespoons are 20ml. Australian readers
should use 3 tsp in place of 1 tbsp for measuring small
quantities of gelatine, cornflour, salt, etc.
Medium eggs are used unless otherwise stated.

Contents

Introduction

Noodles and rice are classic and versatile ingredients. Traditionally they each form the staple element of a meal, and yet there are also innumerable creative ways of reinventing them in a variety of cooking styles, by combining them with other ingredients, spices and flavourings.

it cooks quickly and easily, with little or no advance preparation, it can be used for an astonishing range of sweet and savoury foods, and is easily digested. It is not difficult to see why this grain has continued to grow in popularity.

Rice grains are sourced from aquatic cereal grasses. Originally cultivated mainly in Asia, paddy fields (the word "paddy" refers to the plant that yields the rice) are now a feature of the landscape in Europe and America. Two-thirds of the world's peoples enjoy rice in some form every day, and new varieties are constantly being cultivated.

RICE

Rice is one of the world's oldest and most versatile foods. An excellent source of complex carbohydrates, it is high in fibre, provides useful quantities of B Group vitamins, and contains very little fat. The energy from rice is released slowly into the bloodstream, so it is not a quick-fix carbohydrate like sugar. Considering that

Rice is categorized in most cases as being either long or short grain. Long grain varieties, such as Patna and basmati, tend to retain their shape and remain separate when cooked, whereas the stubbier short grain types cook down to a creamy consistency that makes them the ideal choice for puddings or risottos. The grains of certain short grain types tend to stick together when cooked, an attribute that makes them much sought after for sushi, croquettes or rice cakes. Some varieties, such as Thai rice for example, have characteristics of both types. New varieties and blends appear constantly on our supermarket shelves, giving us every opportunity to expand our repertoire. Two recent arrivals are the red rices from California and the Camargue.

Rice, like pasta, combines perfectly with poultry, fish and shellfish (especially prawns) as well as with vegetables. Vegetarians are amply – and imaginatively – provided for in these rice recipes, with dishes such as Parsnip, Aubergine & Cashew Biryani sharing the limelight with

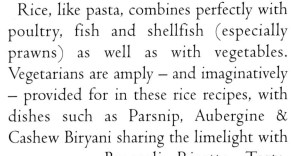

Broccoli Risotto Torte. Remember too, that rice contains no gluten, so a dessert such as Thai Rice Cake is perfect for anyone on a gluten-free diet. Sweet suggestions using rice include a delightful recipe for Moroccan pudding, scented with orange flower water and spiced with cinnamon, and a sundae served with raspberries, nuts and chocolate sauce.

7

NOODLES

Noodles are the original fast food – simple, speedy and satisfying. Their history goes back thousands of years, to the time when man first learned to grind grain. After the discovery that flour could be used to bake bread, it was then a short step to discovering that when it was mixed with

water and pressed or rolled into thin sheets, it could be dried and kept for cooking at a later date.

Long before Marco Polo made his much-vaunted voyages to the Far East, returning with recipes for ravioli and other specialities now almost exclusively associated with Italy, the art of noodle-making had been perfected in the countries of India, Japan, China, Malaysia and present-day Thailand. European cooks, far from sitting back waiting for an enterprising explorer to import this tasty

type of food, were already adding bits of dough to soups and stews. The light and floury dumplings that resulted were known as "nudeln", giving us the word that has become so familiar today.

Oriental noodles are made from a wide variety of grains, including buckwheat and rice, and are often enriched with egg. They may also be of vegetable origin. Cellophane noodles are made from mung beans, and soy beans, chick-peas, corn and even seaweed are just some of the sources of the hundreds of different varieties now available to us. Some types do not even need to be cooked, but are quite simply added to a pan of boiling water and left to stand while the cook swiftly stir-fries some crisp vegetables, and then adds a savoury sauce.

Noodle shops are a familiar part of the street scene in many Oriental cities. In

Bangkok, noodle kiosks cater to city workers' insatiable appetites, while the *klongs* (canals) are thronged with noodle barges. Noodle sellers visit the suburbs, too, trundling their wares on trolleys from house to house. The situation is similar in Vietnam and Korea, while in Japan there are elegant specialist restaurants offering steaming bowls of noodle soup; simply prepared noodles with dipping sauces, and crystal-clear chilled noodle salads featuring beautifully carved vegetables. In many of these restaurants the noodle maker can be seen at work. Unlike his Italian counter-part, he does not roll and cut the dough, but shapes it to a short rope before twisting and whirling it through the air repeatedly to produce the long and slender strands.

As snacks and starters, noodles (and dishes made from noodle dough, such as filled wonton wrappers) come into their own. Spring rolls are one of the most convenient finger foods, providing the perfect way of using up small quantities of meat, fish or vegetables. Fried plain wonton wrappers make delicious crisps for sandwiching simple stir-fried mixtures. Noodle soups, popular the world over, can be either light and delicately flavoured or served as hearty and satisfying main courses.

We've travelled the world to bring you this collection. Dishes range from rissoles to stir fry and from paella to salad, and illustrate the versatility of refreshingly simple ingredients. Whether you sneak a few spring rolls as a light snack, or sit down with the rest of the family to a hearty chicken and prawn jambalaya, rice and noodles both provide endless ways of adding new interest to your menu.

9

Types of Rice

LONG GRAIN WHITE RICE

Perhaps the most familiar type of rice in the West, this is used mainly for savoury dishes. The rice is milled to remove the outer husk of the grain, then polished to remove the bran and give the white grains a sheen.

EASY-COOK RICE

Rice sold as "easy-cook" or "par-boiled" has been treated with high pressure steam before being milled. The steam hardens the outside of the grain, so cooking takes a little longer, but the grains stay separate and are fluffy. Purists claim there is a loss of flavour because of the treatment process.

BASMATI RICE

The name of this rice means "fragrance" in Hindi, and aptly describes this delicately flavoured long grain variety. Basmati rice benefits from being thoroughly rinsed, then soaked for about 10 minutes in cold water, before use. It cooks more quickly than regular long grain rice.

BROWN RICE

This is not a specific type of rice, but a term used to distinguish any grain which retains its bran coating. Also described as wholegrain rice, brown rice has a nutty flavour. Brown rice takes longer to cook than white; some cooks prefer to fry the grains for a minute or two before adding boiling water.

RISOTTO RICE

A collective name for several varieties of short grain rice, all of which cook to a creamy consistency while retaining a bit of "bite". Arborio is the best known type of risotto rice. The secret of a good risotto is lots of patience. The hot liquid must be added gradually, with each ladleful being absorbed before the next is stirred in. The only exception to this rule is paella. Here the stock is added to the rice all at once, and the dish is allowed to simmer without being stirred.

THAI RICES

Thai jasmine and Thai fragrant rice are delicately scented long grain varieties that have a characteristic stickiness when cooked. They cook very quickly and are best cooked with just one-and-a-quarter times the amount of water to rice. Salt is not usually added.

GLUTINOUS RICE

Also called "sticky rice", this term generally refers to a Chinese short grain rice which sticks together on cooking. The name, however, is misleading as the rice does not contain gluten. It is easy to pick up with chopsticks and can be easily shaped and rolled. Glutinous rice can be white or black and is often used for puddings, served with sugar and coconut cream.

SUSHI RICE

As the name suggests, this sticky Japanese short grain rice is used for making sushi, the popular raw fish and rice parcels.

RED RICE

Rice grown in the wild is a light red colour. New varieties which are being bred to recreate this fabulous colouring are now creating considerable interest. For red rice with a buckwheat flavour, try the semi-wild cultivar from the Camargue.

WILD RICE

Not a true rice, but an unrelated aquatic grass from Canada and North America. The long, dark brown grains are costly and take a long time to cook, but the resultant nutty flavour is highly prized. A form of smaller grain, cultivated "wild rice" is cheaper and more easily available. It is often sold blended with long grain rice.

11

Ingredients

CELLOPHANE NOODLES

Sometimes sold as transparent, or glass, noodles, these are clear and shiny. They are generally made from mung bean flour and must be soaked in hot water before cooking. Unlike some oriental noodles, cellophane noodles can be reheated successfully after cooking, and are a favourite ingredient for stir-fries.

EGG NOODLES

Available in skeins or bundles, egg noodles are widely used throughout Asia, and range from very thin strands to narrow ribbons. Both fresh and dried noodles are available, although the latter type is easier to come by. Egg noodles need little cooking: some varieties are simply added to boiling water; others need to be boiled briefly. Always follow the instructions on the packet.

RICE NOODLES

Made from rice flour and water, these long dried noodle strands come in various thicknesses, ranging from very thin to wide ribbons and sheets, and are usually sold in neat bundles, tied with raffia. Fresh rice noodles are also available. Rinse rice noodles in warm water and drain before use. Rice noodles are traditionally served at Chinese birthday celebrations; the longer the strands, the more auspicious the omens for a long and healthy life.

RICE SHEETS

Square or round pieces of rice flour dough, these are used in much the same way as wonton wrappers, to provide a casing for a savoury filling. The sheets are naturally stiff and must be softened before being rolled, either by brushing them with hot water, or by dipping them briefly in hot water.

RICE STICKS

The name is somewhat misleading; rice sticks are simply flat, ribbon-like rice noodles, sold in skeins. As with other rice noodles, they must be soaked in hot water and drained before use.

RICE VERMICELLI

Thin, white and brittle, rice vermicelli is sold in large bundles. When pre-soaked and drained, it cooks almost instantly in hot liquid. Small quantities can also be deep-fried straight from the packet to make a crisp garnish for a soup or a sauce dish.

SOBA

These Japanese noodles are made from buckwheat (or a mixture of buckwheat and wheat flour) and are traditionally cooked in simmering water. Flavoursome and quite chewy, they may be served either hot or cold, with a dipping sauce.

SOMEN

Wheat flour is used to make these delicate white noodles. Like vermicelli, they cook very quickly in boiling water. Somen noodles are sold in dried form, usually tied in bundles that are held together with a paper band.

UDON

Thick and starchy, these noodles are similar to Italian pasta, and can be substituted for linguine. Made from wheat flour and water, they are usually round in shape. A dried wholewheat version is available in some wholefood shops. Udon are also sold fresh, in chilled vacuum packs, or pre-cooked.

WONTON WRAPPERS

It is perfectly possible to make your own wonton dough, but it needs to be rolled wafer-thin and most cooks prefer to buy it as wonton wrappers – neat 7.5cm/3in squares, dusted with cornflour. The wrappers can be frozen for up to six months. They thaw rapidly, ready for filling and frying, steaming or boiling. Wonton wrappers can also be deep-fried, rather like crisps, or used to make spring rolls.

13

Techniques for Rice

RINSING AND SOAKING

Basmati rice and wild rice both benefit from being rinsed in several changes of cold water, then soaked for about 10 minutes before being drained and cooked. The traditional way of rinsing the rice is to add it to a large bowl of water and swirl it gently with your fingers. Glutinous rice is also rinsed and then given a long soak.

COOKING IN AN OPEN PAN

Similar to the method for cooking pasta, this involves adding the rice to a large saucepan of lightly salted boiling water. When the mixture comes back to the boil, stir it once, then leave the rice to cook for 12–15 minutes (10 minutes for basmati or Thai rices). The grains will remain separate. After cooking, drain well, rinsing the rice in boiling water if you like. Leave to stand for 5 minutes before forking up.

COOKING BY ABSORPTION

Rinse the rice if necessary and put it in a saucepan. Add cold water to cover (amounts vary, so check package instructions, but as a general rule 225g/8oz/1 generous cup of long grain rice would require 600ml/1 pint/2½ cups) and add a little salt. Bring to the boil, stir once, then cover tightly and lower the heat so that the rice barely simmers. Cook basmati or Thai rice for 15 minutes; other long grain types for 20 minutes and easy-cook rice for slightly longer. Brown rice will need slightly more water and should be cooked for 25–35 minutes. After cooking, set the pan aside, still covered, for 5 minutes, then fluff up the grains and serve.

QUICK-START BROWN RICE

One way of cooking brown rice is to stir-fry the grains in a little butter before cooking them

in lightly salted boiling water. Use 15g/ ½oz/1 tbsp butter and 600ml/1 pint/2½ cups water for every 225g/8oz/1 cup of brown rice. Having added the water, bring it back to the boil. Stir and cover, then simmer for 35 minutes without lifting the lid. Fork up the grains and serve.

REHEATING

Cooked rice can be kept in the fridge in a sealed container for 2–3 days. To reheat, place the rice in a colander, rinse with boiling water, then set the colander over a saucepan of boiling water. Cover the pan with a cloth and steam for about 15 minutes. To reheat in the microwave, place the rice in a serving dish, cover loosely and heat on High (100% power). Four servings require 2–3 minutes cooking time and the rice should be forked up halfway through.

FAST FLAVOURINGS & QUICK TIPS

• Toss cooked rice with chopped fresh herbs just before serving.

• Fry sliced mushrooms in butter over a high heat until they are tender and most of the liquid has evaporated. Toss into the rice.

• Cook brown rice by the quick-start method, adding a little curry powder when stir-frying the grains. Toss the cooked rice with toasted cashew nuts or almonds or plumped sultanas.

• Make a simple confetti salad by dicing carrots and peppers of various colours very finely and tossing them with freshly cooked and cooled rice. Add a simple vinaigrette.

• Use vegetable stock instead of water for cooking rice by the absorption method.

• Cook rice by the open pan method. Drain but do not rinse with boiling water. Pack the rice in well greased dariole moulds, leave in a warm place for 3–4 minutes, then invert on individual plates. Holding the plate and the mould together, tap firmly on the work surface to release the rice. Lift off the moulds.

• Add bruised green cardamom pods and a cinnamon stick to rice pudding for an oriental flavour. Stir in rosewater just before serving.

15

Techniques

STORING

Store dried noodles in the original packaging in airtight containers in a cool, dry place. They will stay fresh for many months. Fresh noodles (available from the chilled cabinets in oriental food stores) keep for several days in the fridge if sealed in the plastic bag in which they were bought. Check use-by dates. Fresh egg noodles and wonton wrappers can be frozen successfully.

16

PREPARATION

Some noodles, notably cellophane noodles and rice noodles, must be soaked in hot water and drained before use. Follow the instructions in individual recipes. Noodles which are to be cooked twice (parboiled, then stir-fried or simmered in sauce) are initially cooked until they are barely tender, then drained, refreshed under cold running water, and drained again.

If appropriate, they may be tossed with a little oil to prevent any strands from sticking together. At this stage they can be stored in an airtight container in the fridge for several days.

COOKING

Add noodles to a large saucepan of rapidly boiling, lightly salted water, and cook for the time recommended on the packet. Unlike Italian pasta, which should retain a bit of bite, oriental noodles are cooked until they are tender. Avoid overcooking, however, which can make them soggy. Dried noodles are sometimes deep-fried for garnishing or for use as a noodle cake. In this case, do not pre-cook.

Preparing Additional Ingredients

MAKING TAMARIND WATER

Tamarind, the fruit of a tropical tree, is highly valued for its acidic flavour. Sold dry or as pulp, the fruit must be soaked in hot water before use. Mix about 15ml/1 tbsp pulp with 60ml/4 tbsp hot water in a bowl. Leave for 10 minutes, then strain into a clean bowl, pressing the pulp against the sieve to make a thick liquid (tamarind water). Use sparingly.

MAKING COCONUT MILK

To make 250ml/8fl oz/1 cup thick coconut milk (coconut cream), break 115g/4oz/ ½ cup creamed coconut into chunks and place it in a heatproof bowl. Stir in 150ml/¼ pint/⅔ cup boiling water until the coconut is smooth and creamy. If the recipe calls for thin milk, soak 115g/4oz/½ cup creamed coconut in 250ml/8floz/1 cup boiling water in a

blender or food processor for 10 minutes. Process until smooth, then strain before use.

PREPARING LEMON GRASS

Cut off and discard the dry leafy tops, leaving about 15cm/6in of stalk. Peel away any tough outer layers, then lay the lemon grass on a board and bruise it with the flat blade of a cleaver or cook's knife. Cut the lemon grass into thin slices, or chop it finely.

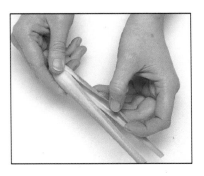

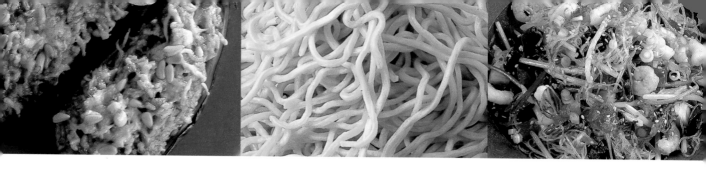

STARTERS, SNACKS AND LIGHT SUPPERS

Sushi

INGREDIENTS

TUNA SUSHI
3 sheets nori (paper-thin seaweed)
150g / 5oz very fresh tuna fillet, cut into thin strips
5ml / 1 tsp wasabi (horseradish mustard), thinned
with water
6 young carrots, blanched
450g / 1lb / 4 cups cooked sushi rice
SALMON SUSHI
4 eggs, lightly beaten
2.5ml / ½ tsp salt
10ml / 2 tsp caster sugar
5 sheets nori
450g / 1lb / 4 cups cooked sushi rice
150g / 5oz very fresh salmon fillet, cut into thin strips
5ml / 1 tsp wasabi, thinned with water
½ small cucumber, cut into 5 batons

SERVES 10–12

1 Make the tuna sushi. Spread half a sheet of nori on a bamboo mat, lay strips of tuna lengthways across and season with the thinned wasabi. Place a blanched carrot next to the tuna and roll tightly. Seal the roll with water.

2 Place a square of non-stick baking paper on the bamboo mat and spread it with sushi rice. Centre the nori roll on top and wrap. Press to set, then cut into rounds. Make more tuna sushi in the same way.

3 Make the salmon sushi. Use the eggs, salt and sugar to make five simple flat omelettes in a non-stick frying pan.

4 Place a sheet of nori on a bamboo mat, cover with an omelette and trim to size. Spread a layer of rice over the omelette, then lay strips of salmon across the width. Spread the salmon lightly with wasabi, then place a cucumber baton next to the salmon. Roll up firmly, then press the roll so that it forms an oval. Cut into slices. Make more salmon sushi in the same way.

20

Rice & Mozzarella Croquettes

INGREDIENTS

115g/4oz/generous ½ cup long grain rice,
freshly boiled
2 eggs, lightly beaten
75g/3oz/½ cup mozzarella cheese, grated
115g/4oz/1 cup dried breadcrumbs
oil, for deep-frying
salt and ground black pepper
fresh dill sprigs, to garnish
AÏOLI
1 egg yolk
few drops of lemon juice
1 large garlic clove, crushed
250ml/8fl oz/1 cup olive oil

MAKES ABOUT 16

1 Drain the cooked rice thoroughly. Cool slightly, then tip into a bowl and stir in the eggs and grated mozzarella, with salt and pepper to taste.

2 Shape the mixture into 16 equal-size balls. Spread out the breadcrumbs in a shallow dish, add the rice balls and shake the dish to coat them thoroughly. Press the crumbs on well and chill the croquettes for 20 minutes.

3 Meanwhile, make the aïoli. Put the egg yolk, lemon juice and garlic into a small, deep bowl. Add salt and pepper to taste. Gradually whisk in the oil, a drop at a time at first, then in a steady stream, until the mixture is thick and glossy. Cover and chill.

4 Deep-fry the rice croquettes in batches in hot oil for 4–5 minutes or until crisp, reheating the oil as necessary. Drain on kitchen paper and keep hot. As soon as all the rice croquettes are cooked, garnish them with dill and serve with the aïoli.

Red Rice Rissoles

INGREDIENTS

25g/1oz/2 tbsp butter
30ml/2 tbsp olive oil
1 large red onion, chopped
1 red pepper, seeded and chopped
2 garlic cloves, crushed
1 fresh red chilli, finely chopped
225g/8oz/generous 1 cup risotto rice
1 litre/1¾ pints/4 cups vegetable stock
4 drained sun-dried tomatoes in oil, chopped
30ml/2 tbsp tomato purée
10ml/2 tsp chopped fresh oregano
45ml/3 tbsp chopped fresh parsley
150g/5oz/1¼ cups Red Leicester cheese, cut into 12 pieces
1 egg, beaten
115g/4oz/1 cup dried breadcrumbs
oil, for deep frying
salt and ground black pepper

SERVES 6

1 Melt the butter in the oil in a large saucepan and fry the onion, pepper, garlic and chilli for 5 minutes. Add the rice and stir-fry for 2 minutes more.

2 Pour in the vegetable stock and add the sun-dried tomatoes, tomato purée and chopped oregano. Season with salt and pepper to taste. Bring to the boil, stirring occasionally, then lower the heat, cover and allow to simmer for 20 minutes.

3 Tip the mixture into a bowl and stir in the chopped parsley. Allow to cool, then chill until firm. When cold, shape the mixture into 12 even-size balls, using your hands. Press a nugget of Red Leicester cheese into the centre of each rice ball.

4 Roll the rice balls in the beaten egg and then coat them in the breadcrumbs. Place the rissoles on a plate and chill again in the fridge for about 30 minutes. Deep fry the rissoles in batches in hot oil for 3–4 minutes, reheating the oil as necessary. Drain the rissoles on kitchen paper and keep hot. Serve with a side salad, if liked.

Stuffed Tomatoes & Peppers

INGREDIENTS

2 ripe beefsteak tomatoes
1 green pepper
1 yellow or orange pepper
60ml/4 tbsp olive oil, plus extra for drizzling
2 onions, chopped
2 garlic cloves, crushed
50g/2oz/½ cup blanched almonds, chopped
*75g/3oz/scant ½ cup long grain rice, boiled
and drained*
30ml/2 tbsp chopped fresh mint
30ml/2 tbsp chopped fresh parsley
45ml/3 tbsp sultanas
150ml/¼ pint/⅔ cup boiling water
45ml/3 tbsp ground almonds
salt and ground black pepper
chopped mixed herbs, to garnish

SERVES 4

1 Preheat the oven to 190°C/375°F/ Gas 5. Cut the tomatoes in half and scoop out the pulp and seeds with a teaspoon. Drain the shells upside-down on  kitchen paper. Chop the tomato flesh roughly.

2 Cut the peppers in half through the stems. Scoop out the seeds. Arrange the peppers, hollows-up, on a baking sheet. Brush with 15ml/1 tbsp of the oil and bake  for 15 minutes. Transfer to a shallow ovenproof dish, add the tomato shells and season with salt and ground black pepper.

3 Heat the remaining oil in a frying pan and fry the onions for 5 minutes until golden. Stir in the garlic and chopped almonds and fry over a medium heat for 1 minute more.

4 Remove the pan from the heat and stir in the rice, chopped tomatoes, mint, parsley and sultanas. Season with salt and pepper and divide the mixture among the tomato and pepper shells.

5 Pour the boiling water around the stuffed vegetables. Bake, uncovered, for 20 minutes, then scatter the ground almonds over the top of the tomatoes and peppers. Drizzle with a little extra olive oil. Bake for 20 minutes more, or until the shells are tender and the rice filling is turning golden. Garnish with the chopped mixed fresh herbs and serve immediately.

Stuffed Vine Leaves with Garlic Yogurt

INGREDIENTS

225g/8oz packet preserved vine leaves
1 onion, finely chopped
4 spring onions, finely chopped
60ml/4 tbsp chopped fresh parsley
10 large mint sprigs, chopped
finely grated rind of 1 lemon
2.5ml/½ tsp crushed dried red chillies
7.5ml/1½ tsp fennel seeds, crushed
175g/6oz/scant 1 cup long grain rice
120ml/4fl oz/½ cup olive oil
300ml/½ pint/1¼ cups boiling water
150ml/¼ pint/⅔ cup thick natural yogurt
2 garlic cloves, crushed
salt
lemon wedges and mint leaves, to garnish
(optional)

SERVES 6

1 Rinse the vine leaves in plenty of cold water. Put into a bowl, cover with boiling water and soak for 10 minutes. Drain well, then dry on kitchen paper.

2 Mix the onion, spring onions, parsley, mint, lemon rind, chillies, fennel seeds and rice in a bowl. Stir in 25ml/1½ tbsp of the olive oil. Season with salt and mix well.

3 Flatten a vine leaf, veins uppermost, on a flat surface. Cut off any stalk. Place a heaped teaspoon of the rice mixture near the stalk end, fold the stalk end over, fold in the sides, then roll up to make a cigar shape. Repeat to make about 28 stuffed leaves.

4 Place any remaining leaves in the bottom of a large heavy-based pan. Arrange the stuffed vine leaves on top in a single layer. Spoon over the remaining oil, then pour in the boiling water.

5 Invert a small plate over the stuffed vine leaves to keep them submerged in the water. Cover the pan and cook over a very low heat for 45 minutes.

6 Meanwhile mix the yogurt and garlic together in a small bowl. Transfer the stuffed leaves to a serving plate. Garnish with lemon wedges and mint, if you like. Serve warm or cold, with the garlic yogurt.

Risotto-stuffed Aubergines

INGREDIENTS

4 small aubergines
105ml/7 tbsp olive oil
1 small onion, chopped
175g/6oz/scant 1 cup risotto rice
750ml/1¼ pints/3 cups vegetable stock
15ml/1 tbsp white wine vinegar
fresh basil sprigs, to garnish
TOPPING
25g/1oz/⅓ cup grated Parmesan cheese
15ml/1 tbsp pine nuts
SPICY TOMATO SAUCE
300ml/½ pint/1¼ cups passata
(puréed tomatoes)
5ml/1 tsp curry paste
pinch of salt

SERVES 4

1 Preheat the oven to 200°C/400°F/Gas 6. Cut the aubergines in half lengthways. Using a sharp knife, cut the flesh criss-cross fashion into neat cubes, then cut round the shells and ease the cubes out. Brush the shells with 30ml/2 tbsp of the oil and place on a baking sheet. Bake for 15 minutes.

2 Heat the rest of the oil in a saucepan. Fry the aubergine cubes with the onion for 3–4 minutes until softened. Stir in the rice and stock and simmer for 15 minutes. Add the vinegar.

3 Raise the oven temperature to 230°C/450°F/ Gas 8. Spoon the rice mixture into the aubergine shells. Sprinkle the Parmesan and pine nuts on top. Bake for 5 minutes to brown the topping.

4 Meanwhile, make the sauce by heating the passata with the curry paste and salt in a small saucepan. Spoon the sauce on to four large plates, position two stuffed aubergine halves on each and garnish with basil sprigs. Serve at once.

Spring Rolls

INGREDIENTS

6 Chinese dried mushrooms, soaked in hot
water for 30 minutes
225g/8oz/1 cup lean minced pork
115g/4oz raw prawns, peeled, deveined and
chopped
115g/4oz white crabmeat, picked over
1 carrot, shredded
50g/2oz cellophane noodles, soaked in
hot water until soft
4 spring onions, finely sliced
2 garlic cloves, finely chopped
30ml/2 tbsp fish sauce
juice of 1 lime
25 x 10cm/4in rice sheets
oil for deep-frying
ground black pepper
lettuce leaves, cucumber slices and
fresh coriander leaves, to garnish

MAKES 25

29

1 Drain the mushrooms and squeeze dry. Remove the stems and slice the caps thinly into a bowl. Add the pork, seafood and carrot. Drain the noodles, snip them into short lengths and add to the bowl with the spring onions and garlic. Stir in the fish sauce and lime juice. Season with pepper and set aside for 30 minutes to allow the flavours to blend.

2 Dip a rice sheet in a bowl of hot water to make it pliable, then lay it on a flat surface. Place about 5cm/2in of the filling near the edge of the rice sheet, fold both ends over, then roll up, sealing the roll with a little water.

3 Heat the oil to 180°C/350°F or until a cube of dried bread browns in 30–45 seconds. Add the rolls a few at a time and fry until golden brown and crisp. Drain  on kitchen paper and serve garnished with lettuce, cucumber and fresh coriander.

Rice Vermicelli & Salad Rolls

INGREDIENTS

*50g/2oz rice vermicelli, soaked in hot water
until soft and drained
1 large carrot, shredded
15ml/1 tbsp granulated sugar
15–30ml/1–2 tbsp fish sauce
8 x 20cm/8in round rice sheets
8 large lettuce leaves, trimmed
350g/12oz/6 cups Chinese roast pork, sliced
115g/4oz/2 cups beansprouts
handful of fresh mint leaves
8 cooked king prawns, peeled, deveined
and halved
½ cucumber, cut into fine strips
fresh coriander leaves*
PEANUT SAUCE
*15ml/1 tbsp vegetable oil
3 garlic cloves, finely chopped
1–2 fresh red chillies, finely chopped
5ml/1 tsp tomato purée
120ml/4fl oz/½ cup water
15ml/1 tbsp smooth peanut butter
30ml/2 tbsp hoisin sauce
2.5ml/½ tsp granulated sugar
juice of 1 lime
50g/2oz/½ cup peanuts, ground*

MAKES 8

30

1 Bring a saucepan of lightly salted water to the boil and cook the vermicelli for 2–3 minutes. Drain, rinse under cold water and drain again. In a bowl, mix the noodles, carrot, sugar and fish sauce.

2 Assemble the rolls one at a time. Dip a rice sheet in a bowl of hot water, then lay it flat. Place a lettuce leaf, 1–2 scoops of the noodle mixture, a few slices of pork, some of the beansprouts and several mint leaves on the rice sheet.

3 Start rolling the rice sheet into a cylinder. When half the sheet has been rolled, fold both sides towards the centre and lay 2 pieces of prawn along the crease. Add a few cucumber strips and coriander leaves, then finish rolling the sheet to make a tight packet. Place on a plate and cover with a damp dish towel while you make the remaining rolls.

4 Make the peanut sauce. Heat the oil in a small saucepan and fry the garlic and chillies for 1 minute. Add the tomato purée and the water and bring to the boil, then stir in the peanut butter, hoisin sauce, sugar and lime juice. Lower the heat and simmer for 3–4 minutes. Spoon the sauce into a bowl, add the ground peanuts and leave to cool.

5 To serve, cut each roll in half widthways to reveal the filling. Arrange on individual plates and add a spoonful of the peanut sauce to each. Garnish with any remaining coriander leaves and beansprouts.

Wonton Crisps with Seared Scallops

INGREDIENTS

16 scallops, halved
oil for deep-frying
8 wonton wrappers
45ml/3 tbsp olive oil
1 large carrot, cut into long thin strips
1 large leek, cut into long thin strips
juice of 1 lemon
juice of ½ orange
2 spring onions, finely sliced
30ml/2 tbsp fresh coriander leaves
salt and ground black pepper
MARINADE
5ml/1 tsp Thai red curry paste
5ml/1 tsp grated fresh root ginger
1 garlic clove, finely chopped
15ml/1 tbsp soy sauce
15ml/1 tbsp olive oil

SERVES 4

1 Make the marinade by mixing all the ingredients in a bowl. Add the scallops, toss to coat, then cover and marinate for 30 minutes. Meanwhile, heat the oil in a large heavy-based saucepan. Deep-fry the wonton wrappers in small batches until crisp and golden. Drain on kitchen paper and set aside.

2 Heat half the olive oil in a large frying pan. Add the scallops, with the marinade, and sear over a high heat for about 1 minute, until golden and just firm to the touch. Using a slotted spoon, transfer the scallops to a plate.

3 Add the remaining olive oil to the pan. When hot, stir-fry the carrot and leek strips until crisp-tender. Season with salt and pepper and stir in the citrus juices.

4 Return the scallops to the pan, mix lightly and warm through. Transfer to a bowl and add the spring onions and fresh coriander. Sandwich a quarter of the mixture between each pair of wonton crisps. Serve at once.

32

Chilli Squid with Noodles

INGREDIENTS

675g/ 1½lb fresh squid
30ml/ 2 tbsp vegetable oil
3 slices of fresh root ginger, peeled and
finely shredded
2 garlic cloves, finely chopped
1 red onion, finely sliced
1 carrot, finely sliced
1 celery stick, sliced diagonally
50g/ 2oz sugar snap peas, topped and tailed
5ml/ 1 tsp granulated sugar
15ml/ 1 tbsp chilli bean paste
2.5ml/ ½ tsp chilli powder
75g/ 3oz cellophane noodles, soaked in hot
water until soft
120ml/ 4fl oz/ ½ cup chicken stock
15ml/ 1 tbsp soy sauce
15ml/ 1 tbsp oyster sauce
5ml/ 1 tsp sesame oil
salt and ground black pepper
fresh coriander, to garnish

SERVES 4

1 Gently pull the squid's head and tentacles from its body. Discard the head; trim and reserve the tentacles. Remove the "quill" from inside the body and peel off the skin. Rub salt into the squid and wash in cold water. Cut the body into rings or squares.

2 Heat the oil in a flameproof casserole. Add the ginger, garlic and onion. Stir-fry for 1–2 minutes, then add the squid, carrot, celery and sugar snap peas. Stir-fry until the squid curls up. Stir in the sugar, chilli bean paste and chilli powder. Transfer the mixture to a bowl and set aside.

3 Drain the noodles. Combine the stock and sauces in the clean casserole. Bring to the boil, add the noodles and cook until tender. Add the squid mixture, cover and cook for 5–6 minutes more, until all the flavours are combined. Season to taste.

4 Serve on heated individual plates. Drizzle sesame oil over each portion and sprinkle with coriander.

33

Sweet & Sour Wonton Wrappers

INGREDIENTS

16–20 *wonton wrappers*
oil for deep-frying
SAUCE
15ml/ 1 tbsp vegetable oil
30ml/ 2 tbsp soft light brown sugar
45ml/ 3 tbsp rice vinegar
15ml/ 1 tbsp light soy sauce
15ml/ 1 tbsp tomato ketchup
45–60ml/ 3–4 tbsp chicken stock
15ml/ 1 tbsp cornflour, mixed to a paste with
a little water

SERVES 4

1 Make the sauce. Heat the oil in a wok or saucepan. Stir in the sugar, rice vinegar, soy sauce, ketchup and stock. Bring to the boil, then add the cornflour  paste, stirring constantly until the sauce is smooth and thick. Lower the heat so that the sauce barely simmers while you cook the wontons.

2 Pinch the centre of each wonton wrapper and twist it around to make the shape of a flower. Heat the oil in a wok or deep-fryer and fry the wonton wrap-  pers for 1–2 minutes, until crisp. Remove with a slotted spoon and drain on kitchen paper.

3 Divide the deep-fried wontons between four plates and spoon a little sauce over each portion. Serve at once, with extra sauce on the side.

34

Fried Cellophane Noodles

INGREDIENTS

175g/6oz cellophane noodles, soaked in hot
water until soft
45ml/3 tbsp vegetable oil
3 garlic cloves, finely chopped
115g/4oz cooked prawns, peeled and deveined
2 lap cheong or other spicy dried sausages,
rinsed, drained and finely diced
2 eggs
2 celery sticks, including leaves, diced
115g/4oz/2 cups beansprouts
115g/4oz spinach leaves, torn into large pieces
2 spring onions, chopped
15–30ml/1–2 tbsp fish sauce
5ml/1 tsp sesame oil
15ml/1 tbsp toasted sesame seeds, to garnish

SERVES 4

1 Drain the noodles, cut them into short lengths and set aside. Heat the vegetable oil in a wok, add the chopped garlic and fry until golden brown. Add the prawns and lap cheong or other diced sausage; stir-fry for 2–3 minutes. Stir in the noodles and fry for 2 minutes more.

2 Make a well in the centre of the prawn mixture, then break in the eggs and stir them gently over a low heat until they are creamy and just set.

3 Add the celery, beansprouts, spinach and spring onions to the wok. Season with fish sauce and add the sesame oil. Toss over the heat until all the ingredients are crisp-tender, then transfer to a serving dish, sprinkle with sesame seeds and serve.

35

Egg Noodles in Soup

INGREDIENTS

225g/8oz skinless, boneless chicken breast
or pork fillet
3–4 Chinese dried mushrooms, soaked in hot
water for 30 minutes
115g/4oz canned sliced bamboo
shoots, drained
115g/4oz young spinach leaves
600ml/1 pint/2½ cups chicken stock
350g/12oz dried egg noodles
30ml/2 tbsp vegetable oil
2 spring onions, thinly sliced
5ml/1 tsp salt
2.5ml/½ tsp soft light brown sugar
15ml/1 tbsp soy sauce
10ml/2 tsp rice wine or dry sherry
few drops of sesame oil

SERVES 4

1 Using a cleaver or sharp knife, shred the meat finely. (If you put the meat in the freezer for 30 minutes before preparing it, it will be much easier to shred.) Drain the mushrooms and squeeze dry. Remove the stems and slice the caps thinly into a bowl. Shred the bamboo shoots and spinach leaves and add them to the bowl.

2 Bring the stock to the boil in a wok or saucepan. Fill a second pan with lightly salted water, bring it to the boil, then cook the egg noodles according to the instructions  on the packet. Drain, rinse under cold water and drain again. Tip into a large serving bowl and pour over the hot stock. Keep the mixture hot.

3 Heat a wok and add the oil. When it is hot, stir-fry the chicken or pork with half the spring onions for 1 minute. Add the mushroom mixture and stir-fry for 2 minutes more or until the meat is cooked.

4 Stir the salt, brown sugar and soy sauce into the wok, with the rice wine or sherry. Toss to mix, heat through for about 30 seconds, then drizzle with the sesame oil.

5 Add the stir-fried mixture to the noodle soup in individual serving bowls, garnish with the remaining finely sliced spring onions and serve.

Malay-Style Soupy Noodles

INGREDIENTS

15ml/ 1 tbsp vegetable oil
2 garlic cloves, very finely chopped
2 shallots, chopped
*900ml/ 1½ pints/ 3¾ cups
chicken stock*
225g/ 8oz lean beef or pork, thinly sliced
150g/ 5oz fish balls
4 raw king prawns, peeled and deveined
350g/ 12oz egg noodles
115g/ 4oz watercress
salt and freshly ground black pepper
GARNISH
115g/ 4oz/ 2 cups beansprouts
2 spring onions, sliced
15ml/ 1 tbsp fresh coriander leaves
2 red chillies, seeded and chopped
30ml/ 2 tbsp deep-fried onions

SERVES 4

1 Heat the oil in a large saucepan and fry the chopped garlic and shallots for 1 minute, then stir in the stock. Bring to the boil, then reduce the heat. Add the beef or pork, fish balls and prawns and simmer for 2 minutes.

2 Bring a large saucepan of water to the boil, add the noodles and cook until tender. Drain them well and divide among individual serving bowls.

3 Season the soup with salt and pepper, then add the watercress. The hot soup will cook it instantly.

4 Using a slotted spoon, scoop out the beef or pork, fish balls, prawns and the watercress from the soup and arrange them over the noodles.
Pour the hot soup over the top. Serve at once, sprinkled with each of the garnishing ingredients.

Spicy Shrimp & Noodle Soup

INGREDIENTS

150g/5oz dried rice noodles, soaked in hot
water until soft
25g/1oz/¼ cup raw cashew nuts
5cm/2in piece of lemon grass, shredded
2 garlic cloves, crushed
1 onion, finely chopped
30ml/2 tbsp vegetable oil
15ml/1 tbsp fish sauce
15ml/1 tbsp mild curry paste
400g/14oz can coconut milk
½ chicken stock cube
450g/1lb white fish fillets, skinned and cut
into bite-size pieces
225g/8oz raw prawns, peeled and deveined
1 small cos lettuce, shredded
115g/4oz/2 cups beansprouts
3 spring onions, shredded
½ cucumber, cut into matchsticks
shrimp crackers, to serve

SERVES 4–6

39

1 Bring a saucepan of lightly salted water to the boil. Add the noodles and cook according to the instructions on the packet. Drain, rinse under cold water and drain again. Using a mortar and pestle, or a food processor, grind the cashew nuts to a paste with the lemon grass, garlic and onion.

2 Heat the oil in a large wok or saucepan, add the nut paste and fry for 1–2 minutes, until the paste begins to brown.

3 Stir in the fish sauce, curry paste and coconut milk. Crumble in the stock cube. Simmer for 10 minutes, then place the fish and prawns in a large frying basket, immerse in the simmering liquid and cook for 3–4 minutes.

4 Line a large platter with the shredded lettuce. Arrange the beansprouts, spring onions, cucumber, fish, prawns, noodles and shrimp crackers in separate piles on top. Ladle the soup into bowls and invite guests to add their own accompaniments.

Noodles with Ginger

INGREDIENTS

handful of fresh coriander sprigs
225g/8oz dried egg noodles
45ml/3 tbsp groundnut oil
5cm/2in piece of fresh root ginger, peeled
and cut into fine shreds
6–8 spring onions, cut into shreds
30ml/2 tbsp light soy sauce
salt and ground black pepper

SERVES 4

40

1 Strip the leaves from the coriander stalks. Pile the leaves on a chopping board and chop them quite coarsely with a cleaver or sharp kitchen knife.

2 Cook the noodles according to the instructions on the packet. Drain, rinse under cold water and drain again. Tip into a bowl and toss with 15ml/1 tbsp of the oil.

3 Heat a wok, add the remaining oil and swirl it around. Stir-fry the ginger for a few seconds, then add the noodles and spring onions. Stir-fry for 3–4 minutes, until the spring onions are crisp-tender and the noodles are heated through.

4 Sprinkle the soy sauce and chopped fresh coriander over the noodles. Add salt and pepper to taste and toss over the heat for about 30 seconds more. Serve at once.

Chicken, Vermicelli & Egg Shred Soup

INGREDIENTS

3 large eggs
30ml/ 2 tbsp chopped fresh coriander
1.5 litres/ 2½ pints/ 6¼ cups chicken stock
115g/ 4oz vermicelli, broken into short lengths
115g/ 4oz cooked chicken, sliced
salt and ground black pepper

SERVES 4–6

1 Whisk the eggs in a small bowl and stir in the chopped coriander. Heat a small non-stick frying pan and pour in 30–45ml/ 2–3 tbsp of the mixture, swirling to cover the bottom of the pan. Cook until set, then slide the omelette on to a board. Repeat until all the egg mixture is used up. Roll each omelette up. Using a sharp knife, slice thinly into shreds and set aside.

2 Bring the stock to the boil in a large saucepan. Add the vermicelli. Cook for 3–5 minutes, until almost tender, then add the chicken. Season with salt and black pepper and cook for 2–3 minutes, until the chicken is heated through.

3 Stir in the egg shreds and serve immediately, in heated individual bowls.

41

Stir-fried Noodles with Spinach

INGREDIENTS

15ml/ 1 tbsp sunflower oil
2.5cm/ 1in piece of fresh root ginger, grated
2 garlic cloves, crushed
45ml/ 3 tbsp dark soy sauce
150ml/ ¼ pint/ ⅔ cup boiling water
225g/ 8oz/ 2 cups peas, thawed if frozen
450g/ 1lb dried rice noodles
450g/ 1lb spinach leaves, coarse stalks removed
30ml/ 2 tbsp smooth peanut butter
30ml/ 2 tbsp tahini
150ml/ ¼ pint/ ⅔ cup milk
1 ripe avocado
roasted peanuts and peeled, cooked prawns,
to garnish

SERVES 6

1 Heat a wok and add the oil. When the oil is hot, stir-fry the ginger and garlic for 30 seconds. Add 15ml/ 1 tbsp of the soy sauce, then stir in the boiling water.

2 Add the peas and noodles to the wok, cook for 3 minutes, then add the spinach leaves. Toss over the heat for 1–2 minutes more, until the spinach is wilted and the noodles are tender, then drain the mixture and keep it hot.

3 Wipe out the wok and add the peanut butter, tahini and milk. Stir in the remaining 30ml/2 tbsp soy sauce and mix well. Bring to the boil and simmer for 1 minute. Meanwhile, cut the avocado in half, remove the stone and peel and slice the flesh neatly.

4 Return the pea, noodle and spinach mixture to the wok, with the avocado slices. Toss gently to mix and heat through. Serve on individual plates, with some of the peanut and tahini sauce spooned over each portion. Garnish with roasted peanuts and peeled, cooked prawns.

42

MEAT AND
POULTRY DISHES

Rice, Beef & Broad Bean Koftas

INGREDIENTS

115g/4oz/generous ½ cup long grain rice
450g/1lb lean minced beef
115g/4oz/1 cup plain flour
3 eggs, beaten
115g/4oz/1 cup podded broad beans, thawed
if frozen, skinned
30ml/2 tbsp chopped fresh dill
25g/1oz/2 tbsp butter
1 large onion, chopped
2.5ml/½ tsp ground turmeric
1.2 litres/2 pints/5 cups water
salt and ground black pepper
chopped fresh parsley, to garnish
naan bread, to serve

SERVES 4

1 Bring a saucepan of lightly salted water to the boil. Add the rice and par-cook for 4 minutes, then drain thoroughly. Tip into a bowl and add the minced beef, flour and eggs, with salt and pepper to taste. Knead until well blended.

2 Add the skinned broad beans and dill. Knead again until the mixture is firm and pasty. Shape into eight large balls, place on a plate and chill for 15 minutes.

3 Melt the butter in a large saucepan and fry the onion for 3–4 minutes until golden. Stir in the turmeric, cook for 30 seconds, then add the water. Bring to the boil.

4 Add the meat-balls to the pan. Lower the heat and simmer for 45–60 minutes, until the meatballs are fully cooked and the sauce has reduced to about 250ml/

8fl oz/1 cup. Tip the mixture into a serving dish, garnish with the parsley and serve with naan.

Thai Fried Rice with Pork

INGREDIENTS

45ml/3 tbsp corn oil
1 onion, chopped
2–3 garlic cloves, chopped
115g/4oz tender boneless pork, cubed
2 eggs, beaten
450g/1lb/4 cups cooked rice
30ml/2 tbsp fish sauce
15ml/1 tbsp dark soy sauce
2.5ml/½ tsp caster sugar
GARNISH
4 spring onions, finely sliced
2 fresh red chillies, sliced
1 lime, cut into wedges
1 small omelette, cut into strips

SERVES 4

1 Heat the oil in a wok or large frying pan. Stir-fry the onion with the garlic until softened, then add the pork and stir-fry until it is fully cooked.

2 Pour in the beaten eggs, stirring them into the pork mixture with a wooden spatula. Continue to stir over the heat until the eggs are scrambled.

3 Add the rice and stir gently to coat. Toss the mixture over the heat, taking care to prevent the rice from sticking to the pan.

4 Add the sauces and sugar. Mix well. When the rice is hot, tip the mixture into warmed individual serving bowls. Garnish with the spring onions,

chillies and lime wedges and arrange the strips of omelette on top. Serve at once.

Turkish Lamb Pilau

INGREDIENTS

40g / 1½oz / 3 tbsp butter
1 large onion, finely chopped
450g / 1lb lamb fillet, trimmed and cut into small cubes
2.5ml / ½ tsp ground cinnamon
30ml / 2 tbsp tomato purée
45ml / 3 tbsp chopped fresh parsley
115g / 4oz / ½ cup ready-to-eat dried apricots, halved
75g / 3oz / ¾ cup pistachio nuts, chopped
450g / 1lb / 2¼ cups long grain rice, rinsed
salt and ground black pepper
flat leaf parsley, to garnish

SERVES 4

2 Add the tomato purée to the pan, then add enough water to cover the meat. Stir in the chopped fresh parsley. Bring to the boil, lower the heat, cover the pan and allow to simmer gently for 1½ hours or until the meat is tender.

3 Add enough water to the pan to make the liquid up to about 600ml/1 pint/2½ cups. Stir in the apricots, pistachios and rice. Bring to the boil, lower the heat, cover tightly and simmer for 20 minutes, or until the rice is cooked and the liquid has been absorbed. Taste the pilau and adjust the seasoning.

4 Spoon the pilau into a warmed serving dish and garnish with the flat leaf parsley. Serve at once.

1 Heat the butter in a large heavy-based pan. Add the onion and cook until soft and golden. Move the onion to the side of the pan and add the lamb

cubes. Brown on all sides, then sprinkle with the cinnamon and season with pepper. Stir, cover and cook gently for 10 minutes.

COOK'S TIP

It is important that the meat retains its tenderness. Check the lamb from time to time while it is cooking, and add more water if necessary.

French Beans, Rice & Beef

INGREDIENTS

25g / 1oz / 2 tbsp butter
1 large onion, chopped
450g / 1lb braising steak, cubed
2 garlic cloves, crushed
5ml / 1 tsp each ground cinnamon, cumin
and turmeric
450g / 1lb tomatoes, chopped
30ml / 2 tbsp tomato purée
350ml / 12fl oz / 1½ cups water
350g / 12oz French beans, trimmed and halved
salt and ground black pepper
RICE
275g / 10oz / 1½ cups basmati rice, soaked
40g / 1½oz / 3 tbsp butter
2–3 saffron strands, soaked in 15ml / 1 tbsp
boiling water

SERVES 4

1 Melt the butter in a large heavy-based pan and fry the onion until golden. Move it aside and brown the beef cubes, then stir in the garlic, spices, tomatoes, tomato purée and water. Season with salt and pepper. Bring to the boil, lower the heat and simmer for 30 minutes, then add the beans and cook for 15 minutes more, until the meat is tender and most of the liquid has evaporated.

2 Cook the drained rice in lightly salted boiling water for 5 minutes. Lower the heat and simmer for 10 minutes, then drain, rinse under hot water and drain again.

3 Melt 15g/½oz/1 tbsp of the butter in the clean pan. Stir in a third of the rice. Spread about half the meat mixture on top. Continue to layer the mixtures until all are used, ending with rice. Melt the remaining butter and drizzle it over. Cover tightly and steam for 30–45 minutes over a low heat.

4 Spoon 45ml/3 tbsp of the rice into a bowl and stir in the strained saffron liquid. Pile the remaining rice and beef mixture into a warmed serving dish, sprinkle the saffron rice on top and serve.

50

Chicken & Prawn Jambalaya

INGREDIENTS

50g / 2oz / 4 tbsp lard
2 chickens, about 1.5kg / 3–3½lb each, jointed
450g / 1lb raw smoked gammon, rinded and diced
3 onions, finely sliced
50g / 2oz / ½ cup plain flour
2 x 400g / 14oz cans chopped tomatoes
2 green peppers, seeded and sliced
2–3 garlic cloves, crushed
10ml / 2 tsp chopped fresh thyme
500g / 1¼lb / 3 cups long grain rice
1.2 litres / 2 pints / 5 cups water
2–3 dashes of Tabasco sauce
24 raw Mediterranean prawns, peeled and
deveined, tails left intact
6 spring onions, finely chopped
45ml / 3 tbsp chopped fresh parsley
salt and ground black pepper

SERVES 8–10

1 Melt the lard in a large heavy-based pan. Fry the chicken pieces, gammon and onions, turning occasionally, for 15–20 minutes, until the chicken is golden brown on all sides. Using a slotted spoon, transfer the mixture to a dish.

2 Lower the heat, sprinkle the flour into the fat remaining in the pan and cook, stirring constantly, until the mixture is pale golden. Stir in the chopped

tomatoes, green peppers, garlic and thyme. Cook, stirring, until the mixture forms a thick sauce, then return the chicken mixture to the pan and cook for 10 minutes, stirring occasionally.

3 Stir in the rice, with salt and pepper to taste. Pour in the water, add the Tabasco and bring to the boil. Lower the heat, add the prawns and cook until the prawns are pink and the rice has absorbed the liquid. Both chicken and rice should be tender.

4 Stir in the spring onions with 30ml / 2 tbsp of the chopped parsley. Spoon the jambalaya on to a heated serving platter, garnish with the remaining chopped parsley and serve at once.

51

Yogurt Chicken & Rice

INGREDIENTS

40g/1½oz/3 tbsp butter
1.5kg/3–3½lb chicken
1 large onion, chopped
250ml/8fl oz/1 cup chicken stock
2 eggs
475ml/16fl oz/2 cups natural yogurt
2–3 saffron strands, soaked in 15ml/1 tbsp
boiling water
5ml/1 tsp ground cinnamon
450g/1lb/2¼ cups basmati rice, soaked
75g/3oz/½ cup zereshk or redcurrants
salt and ground black pepper
herb salad, to serve

SERVES 6

1 Melt 25g/1oz/2 tbsp of the butter in a large flameproof casserole. Add the chicken, with the chopped onion. Cook, turning the chicken frequently, until it is browned on all sides and the onion has softened.

2 Add the stock, with seasoning if needed. Bring to the boil, lower the heat and simmer for 45 minutes or until the chicken is cooked and the stock has reduced by half.

3 Drain the chicken, reserving the stock, and remove the skin and bones. Cut the flesh into large pieces and place in a large bowl.

4 Beat the eggs with the yogurt, strained saffron water and cinnamon. Add salt and pepper to taste. Pour over the chicken, stir to coat, then marinate for up to 2 hours.

5 Cook the drained rice in lightly salted boiling water for 5 minutes. Lower the heat and simmer for 10 minutes, then drain, rinse under hot water and drain again. Lift the chicken pieces out of the marinade and set them aside. Stir half the rice into the yogurt marinade.

6 Preheat the oven to 160°C/325°F/Gas 3. Grease a large ovenproof dish, about 10cm/4in deep. Spread the rice and yogurt mixture on the base, arrange the chicken pieces on top and then add the plain rice. Sprinkle with the berries.

7 Pour over the reserved chicken stock, dot with the remaining butter, cover tightly with foil and bake for 35–45 minutes.

8 Remove the dish from the oven and place on a cold, dampened dish towel for a few minutes. Run a knife around the inner rim, invert a platter on top of the dish and turn the rice "cake" out. Serve in wedges, with a herb salad.

Chicken Biryani

INGREDIENTS

30ml / 2 tbsp oil
1 onion, thinly sliced
2 garlic cloves, crushed
1 fresh green chilli, finely chopped
15ml / 1 tbsp finely chopped fresh root ginger
*675g / 1½lb chicken breasts, skinned, boned
and cubed*
45ml / 3 tbsp curry paste
1.5ml / ¼ tsp salt
1.5ml / ¼ tsp garam masala
3 tomatoes, cut into thin wedges
275g / 10oz / 1½ cups basmati rice, soaked
1.5ml / ¼ tsp ground turmeric
2 bay leaves
4 green cardamom pods
4 cloves
6 cashew nuts

SERVES 4

1 Preheat the oven to 190°C/375°F/Gas 5. Heat the oil in a large frying pan. Fry the onion for 5–7 minutes, until lightly browned. Add the garlic, chilli and ginger and fry for 2 minutes more. Add the chicken and fry for 5 minutes, stirring.

2 Stir in the curry paste, salt and garam masala. Cook for 5 minutes. Add the tomatoes and cook for 3–4 minutes more. Remove from the heat.

3 Bring a large saucepan of lightly salted water to the boil. Add the drained rice and the turmeric. Cook for 10 minutes or until the rice is almost tender. Drain, tip into a bowl and toss with the bay leaves, cardamoms, cloves and cashew nuts.

4 Layer the rice and chicken mixture in a shallow ovenproof dish, finishing with a layer of rice. Cover the dish with foil and bake in the oven for about 15 minutes, or until the chicken is tender. Serve hot.

Chicken & Vermicelli Stir-fry

INGREDIENTS

120ml/4fl oz/½ cup vegetable oil
225g/8oz dried rice vermicelli, broken into short lengths
150g/5oz French beans, topped, tailed and cut in half lengthways
1 onion, finely chopped
2 skinless, boneless chicken breasts, about 175g/6oz each, cut into strips
5ml/1 tsp chilli powder
225g/8oz cooked prawns, peeled and deveined
45ml/3 tbsp dark soy sauce
45ml/3 tbsp white wine vinegar
10ml/2 tsp caster sugar
fresh coriander sprigs, to garnish

SERVES 4

1 Heat a wok and add 60ml/4 tbsp of the oil. When hot, add the vermicelli in batches and fry until crisp. Remove with a slotted spoon and keep hot.

2 Heat the remaining oil in the wok, then add the French beans, onion and chicken. Stir-fry for about 3 minutes, until the chicken is cooked, then sprinkle in the chilli powder and toss over the heat for 1 minute more.

3 Add the prawns, soy sauce, white wine vinegar and caster sugar. Stir-fry for 2 minutes. Strew the fried vermicelli around the rims of four individual plates and pile a portion of the chicken mixture in the centre of each. Garnish with fresh coriander sprigs and serve at once.

Noodles with Spicy Meatballs

INGREDIENTS

350g/12oz dried egg noodles
45ml/3 tbsp sunflower oil
1 onion, thinly sliced
2 garlic cloves, crushed
5cm/2in piece of fresh root ginger, peeled and
cut into thin matchsticks
1.2 litres/2 pints/5 cups chicken stock
30ml/2 tbsp dark soy sauce
2 celery sticks, thinly sliced, leaves reserved
6 Chinese cabbage leaves, cut into
bite-size pieces
50g/2oz mangetouts, trimmed and cut
into strips
SPICY MEATBALLS
450g/1lb/2 cups minced beef
1 large onion, finely chopped
2 fresh red chillies, seeded and finely chopped
2 garlic cloves, crushed
15ml/1 tbsp ground coriander
5ml/1 tsp ground cumin
10ml/2 tsp dark soy sauce
5ml/1 tsp soft dark brown sugar
juice of ½ lemon
salt and ground black pepper
beaten egg, for binding
oil, for shallow frying

SERVES 6

1 Make the meatballs by putting all the ingredients except the oil in a large bowl and mixing thoroughly. Use only enough beaten egg to bind the mixture. Shape into small, evenly sized balls.

2 Bring a saucepan of lightly salted water to the boil and cook the noodles according to the instructions on the packet. Drain, rinse under cold water and drain again.

3 Heat the oil in a large shallow pan and fry the onion, garlic and ginger until softened. Pour in the stock and soy sauce and bring to the boil.

4 Add the meat-balls to the pan, then lower the heat and simmer, partially covered, for 5 minutes. Add the celery slices, simmer for 2 minutes more,  then add the Chinese cabbage and mangetouts. Simmer for 1 minute or until the meatballs are fully cooked.

5 Divide the noodles between six heated soup bowls. Add meatballs and vegetables to each bowl, then ladle stock on top. Garnish with the reserved celery leaves and serve.

56

Cellophane Noodles with Pork

INGREDIENTS

*225g/8oz pork fillet, trimmed and cut into
very small cubes
30ml/2 tbsp dark soy sauce
30ml/2 tbsp rice wine or dry sherry
2 garlic cloves, crushed
15ml/1 tbsp grated fresh root ginger
5ml/1 tsp chilli oil
115g/4oz cellophane noodles, soaked in hot
water until soft
4 Chinese dried mushrooms, soaked in hot
water for 30 minutes
45ml/3 tbsp groundnut oil
4–6 spring onions, chopped
5ml/1 tsp cornflour, mixed with 175ml/
6fl oz/¾ cup chicken stock
30ml/2 tbsp chopped fresh coriander
salt and ground black pepper, to taste
fresh coriander sprigs, to garnish*

SERVES 3–4

1 Put the pork in a bowl with the soy sauce, rice wine or sherry, garlic, ginger and chilli oil. Mix well, then cover and marinate for about 15 minutes.

2 Drain the noodles. Snip them into 13cm/5in lengths. Drain the mushrooms and squeeze dry. Remove the stems and chop the caps finely. Drain the pork, reserving the marinade.

3 Heat a wok and add the oil. When hot, stir-fry the pork and mushrooms for 3 minutes. Add the spring onions and toss over the heat for 1 minute more, then stir in the cornflour mixture with the reserved marinade. Cook for 1 minute, stirring.

4 Add the noodles and stir-fry for 2 minutes, until they have absorbed most of the liquid and the pork is cooked. Stir in the chopped fresh coriander, salt and pepper. Serve garnished with coriander sprigs.

Three-Meat Noodles

INGREDIENTS

450g/1lb dried egg noodles
1 skinless, boneless chicken breast
115g/4oz pork fillet, trimmed
115g/4oz lamb's liver
2 eggs
90ml/6 tbsp vegetable oil
25g/1oz/2 tbsp butter
2 garlic cloves, crushed
115g/4oz cooked prawns, peeled and deveined
115g/4oz young spinach leaves
2 celery sticks, thinly sliced
4 spring onions, finely chopped
60ml/4 tbsp chicken stock
dark soy sauce
salt and ground black pepper
deep-fried onions and celery leaves, to garnish

SERVES 6

1 Bring a saucepan of lightly salted water to the boil and cook the noodles. Drain, rinse under cold water and drain again.

2 Slice the chicken, pork and lamb's liver finely and set aside. Beat the eggs with salt and pepper to taste. Heat 5ml/1 tsp oil with the butter in a small frying pan. Stir in the eggs and cook over a low heat, stirring constantly until scrambled. Set aside.

3 Heat a wok, then add the remaining oil. Stir-fry the chicken, pork and liver with the garlic for 2–3 minutes, until the liver has changed colour. Add the prawns, spinach, celery and spring onions and toss over the heat for 2 minutes.

4 Add the drained noodles to the pan and toss again to mix. Moisten with the stock and add soy sauce to taste. Stir in the scrambled egg and serve, garnished with deep-fried onions and celery leaves.

Stir-fried Rice Noodles with Chicken & Prawns

INGREDIENTS

225g/8oz dried flat rice noodles, soaked in hot
water until soft
120ml/4fl oz/½ cup water
60ml/4 tbsp fish sauce
15ml/1 tbsp granulated sugar
15ml/1 tbsp freshly squeezed lime juice
5ml/1 tsp paprika
pinch of cayenne pepper
45ml/3 tbsp vegetable oil
2 garlic cloves, crushed
1 skinless, boneless chicken breast, thinly sliced
8 raw prawns, peeled, deveined and cut
in half lengthways
1 egg
50g/2oz/½ cup roasted peanuts,
coarsely crushed
3 spring onions, cut into short lengths
175g/6oz/3 cups beansprouts
fresh coriander leaves and lime wedges,
to garnish

SERVES 4

1 Drain the noodles, tip them into a bowl and set aside. Mix the water, fish sauce, sugar, lime juice, paprika and cayenne in a small bowl.

2 Heat a wok, add the oil, then fry the garlic for 30 seconds. Add the chicken slices and prawns and stir-fry for 3–4 minutes. Sweep the chicken mixture to the sides of the wok and add the egg to the centre. Cook the egg, stirring it constantly, until it is lightly scrambled.

3 Add the drained noodles and the fish sauce mixture to the wok. Mix well, then add half the crushed, roasted peanuts. Toss over the heat until the noodles are soft and most of the liquid has been absorbed.

4 Add the spring onions and two-thirds of the beansprouts to the wok. Toss over the heat for 1 minute more, then spoon on to a large serving platter and sprinkle with the remaining peanuts and beansprouts. Garnish with the fresh coriander and lime wedges and serve.

60

Noodles with Beef & Black Bean Sauce

INGREDIENTS

15ml/ 1 tbsp cornflour
30ml/ 2 tbsp soy sauce
30ml/ 2 tbsp oyster sauce
15ml/ 1 tbsp chilli black bean sauce
120ml/ 4fl oz/ ½ cup vegetable stock
60ml/ 4 tbsp vegetable oil
1 onion, thinly sliced
2 garlic cloves, crushed
2 slices of fresh root ginger, peeled and finely chopped
225g/ 8oz mixed peppers, seeded and sliced into strips
350g/ 12oz rump steak, finely sliced against the grain
45ml/ 3 tbsp fermented black beans, rinsed in hot water, drained and chopped
450g/ 1lb fresh rice noodles, rinsed in hot water and drained
2 spring onions, finely chopped, and 2 fresh red chillies, seeded and finely sliced, to garnish

SERVES 4

1 Put the cornflour in a small bowl. Stir in the soy sauce, oyster sauce and chilli black bean sauce, then add the stock and stir until smooth. Set aside.

2 Heat a wok and add half the oil. Stir-fry the onion, garlic, ginger and strips of mixed pepper for 3–5 minutes. Remove with a slotted spoon. Keep hot.

3 Heat the remaining oil in the wok. Stir-fry the steak with the fermented black beans over a high heat for 5 minutes. Return the stir-fried vegetables to the wok, add the cornflour mixture and cook, stirring, for 1 minute.

4 Add the noodles to the wok and toss over a medium heat until cooked. Taste, and add more soy sauce, if necessary. Tip the noodles into a heated bowl

and serve, garnished with the chopped spring onions and fresh chillies.

Pork Satay with Crisp Noodle Cake

INGREDIENTS

3 garlic cloves, crushed
15ml/1 tbsp Thai curry powder
5ml/1 tsp ground cumin
5ml/1 tsp granulated sugar
15ml/1 tbsp fish sauce
90ml/6 tbsp vegetable oil
450g/1lb lean pork, cut into 5cm/2in strips
350g/12 oz dried egg noodles, cooked, rinsed
and drained
fresh coriander leaves, to garnish
SATAY SAUCE
30ml/2 tbsp vegetable oil
2 garlic cloves, finely chopped
1 small onion, finely chopped
2.5ml/½ tsp hot chilli powder
5ml/1 tsp Thai curry powder
250ml/8fl oz/1 cup coconut milk
15ml/1 tbsp fish sauce
30ml/2 tbsp granulated sugar
30ml/2 tbsp lemon juice
165g/5½oz/½ cup peanut butter

SERVES 4

1 Mix the garlic, spices, sugar, fish sauce and 30ml/2 tbsp vegetable oil in a bowl. Add the meat, toss to coat, then cover and marinate for at least 2 hours. Soak eight bamboo skewers in cold water.

2 Make the satay sauce. Heat the oil in a heavy-based saucepan and fry the garlic and onion for 1 minute. Stir in the spices and fry for 2 minutes. Add the remaining ingredients. Mix well. Cook over a low heat for 20 minutes, stirring frequently, until the sauce thickens.

3 Heat 15ml/1 tbsp of the remaining oil in a large frying pan. Spread the noodles in the pan and fry for 4–5 minutes until crisp and golden. Turn the noodle cake over carefully and cook the other side. Keep hot. Preheat the grill or light the barbecue.

4 Drain the meat and thread it neatly on to the drained skewers. Cook over medium coals or under the grill for 8–10 minutes, turning occasionally and brushing the satays with oil. Transfer to a platter, garnish with fresh coriander and serve with wedges of noodle cake and the satay sauce.

Noodle & Cabbage Rolls

INGREDIENTS

4 Chinese dried mushrooms, soaked in hot
water for 30 minutes
50g/2oz cellophane noodles, soaked in hot
water until soft and drained
450g/1lb/2 cups minced pork
4 spring onions, finely chopped
2 garlic cloves, finely chopped
30ml/2 tbsp fish sauce
12 large outer leaves of green cabbage
4 spring onions
30ml/2 tbsp vegetable oil
1 small onion, finely chopped
2 garlic cloves, crushed
400g/14oz can chopped tomatoes
pinch of granulated sugar
salt and ground black pepper

SERVES 4

65

vegetables under cold water and drain. Pat dry with kitchen paper. Split each spring onion into ribbons by cutting through the bulb and tearing upwards.

1 Drain the mushrooms and squeeze dry. Remove the stems and chop the caps. Place them in a bowl. Snip the noodles into short lengths and add them to the bowl with the pork, spring onions and garlic. Season with the fish sauce and mix well.

2 Cut out the stem from each cabbage leaf. Bring a pan of water to the boil and blanch the leaves and whole spring onions for 1 minute. Refresh the

3 Place a spoonful of the pork filling in the centre of each cabbage leaf. Roll up the leaf to make a neat parcel. Tie each roll with a spring onion ribbon.

4 Heat the oil in a large frying pan and fry the onion and garlic over a low heat for 5 minutes. Stir in the tomatoes, with salt, pepper and sugar to taste. Heat gently, then add the cabbage parcels. Simmer, covered, for 20–25 minutes, or until the cabbage rolls are fully cooked. Serve hot.

Braised Birthday Noodles

INGREDIENTS

1kg/ 2¼lb lean neck fillet of lamb, cut into
5cm/ 2in thick medallions
30ml/ 2 tbsp vegetable oil
350g/ 12oz dried thick egg noodles
15ml/ 1 tbsp cornflour
30ml/ 2 tbsp soy sauce
15ml/ 1 tbsp hoisin sauce
30ml/ 2 tbsp rice wine or dry sherry
grated rind and juice of ½ orange
15ml/ 1 tbsp red wine vinegar
5ml/ 1 tsp soft light brown sugar
115g/ 4oz fine green beans, trimmed
and blanched
salt and ground black pepper
2 halved hard-boiled eggs and chopped spring
onions, to garnish
MARINADE
2 garlic cloves, crushed
10ml/ 2 tsp grated fresh root ginger
30ml/ 2 tbsp soy sauce
30ml/ 2 tbsp rice wine or dry sherry
1–2 dried red chillies
30ml/ 2 tbsp vegetable oil

SERVES 4

1 Mix together all the ingredients for the marinade in a large shallow dish. Add the lamb medallions, turn to coat, and marinate for at least 4 hours or overnight.

2 Heat the oil in a large heavy-based saucepan. Fry the lamb for 5 minutes, until it is browned, then add just enough water to cover. Bring to the boil, skim, then lower the heat and simmer for 40 minutes or until tender, adding more water if necessary.

3 Bring a large saucepan of lightly salted water to the boil. Add the noodles and cook for 1 minute only. Drain, rinse under cold water and drain again. Set aside.

4 Mix the cornflour with the soy sauce and hoisin sauce, rice wine or sherry, orange rind and juice, vinegar and brown sugar. Add to the lamb and cook, stirring, until the sauce thickens.

5 Add the noodles and beans. Simmer, stirring occasionally, until both are fully cooked. Season and serve in individual bowls, garnished with the hard-boiled eggs and chopped spring onions.

Fragrant Chicken Curry with Vermicelli

INGREDIENTS

1 chicken, about 1.4–1.6kg/ 3–3½lb
225g/ 8oz sweet potatoes
60ml/ 4 tbsp vegetable oil
1 onion, thinly sliced
3 garlic cloves, crushed
30–45ml/ 2–3 tbsp Thai curry powder
5ml/ 1 tsp granulated sugar
10ml/ 2 tsp fish sauce
1 lemon grass stalk, cut in half
600ml/ 1 pint/ 2½ cups coconut milk
*350g/ 12oz rice vermicelli, soaked in hot
water until soft*
lemon wedges, to serve
GARNISH
115g/ 4oz/ 2 cups beansprouts
2 spring onions, sliced diagonally
2 fresh red chillies, sliced diagonally
8–10 fresh mint leaves

SERVES 4

1 Skin the chicken. Cut the flesh into small pieces and set it aside. Peel the sweet potatoes and cut them into chunks, about the same size as the pieces of chicken.

2 Heat half the vegetable oil in a heavy-based saucepan and fry the onion and garlic over a low heat for 5 minutes. Push the onion and garlic to the side of the pan and stir-fry the chicken pieces until they change colour.

3 Stir in the curry powder, cook for 1 minute, then add the sugar, fish sauce and lemon grass. Pour in the coconut milk and cook over a low heat for about 15 minutes.

4 Meanwhile, heat the remaining oil in a large frying pan and fry the sweet potatoes until they turn pale gold. Using a slotted spoon, remove them from the pan and add them to the chicken mixture. Cook for 15 minutes more, until both the chicken and the sweet potatoes are tender.

5 Drain the vermicelli. Bring a saucepan of lightly salted water to the boil and cook the vermicelli for 2–3 minutes, until tender. Drain, then divide between four individual shallow bowls and top with the chicken curry. Garnish with beansprouts, spring onions, chillies and mint leaves, and serve with lemon wedges.

FISH AND
SEAFOOD DISHES

Rice & Prawn Layer

INGREDIENTS

2 large onions, sliced and deep-fried
300ml / ½ pint / 1¼ cups natural yogurt
30ml / 2 tbsp tomato purée
60ml / 4 tbsp green masala paste
30ml / 2 tbsp lemon juice
5ml / 1 tsp cumin seeds
5cm / 2in piece of cinnamon stick
4 green cardamom pods
450g / 1lb raw king prawns, peeled and deveined
225g / 8oz / 2 cups small button mushrooms
175g / 6oz / generous 1 cup thawed frozen peas
450g / 1lb / 2¼ cups basmati rice, soaked
300ml / ½ pint / 1¼ cups water
3–4 saffron strands, soaked in 90ml / 6 tbsp milk
25g / 1oz / 2 tbsp ghee (clarified butter)
salt

SERVES 4–6

1 Mix the onions, yogurt, tomato purée, masala, lemon juice, cumin seeds, cinnamon, cardamoms and a little salt in a bowl. Stir in the prawns, mushrooms and peas. Mix well, cover and set aside in a cool place for 2 hours.

2 Grease the bottom of a heavy-based frying pan and add the prawn mixture, with any juices. Drain the rice and spread it evenly on top.

3 Pour the water all over the surface of the rice. Using a spoon handle, make random holes through the rice. Strain the saffron milk and spoon a little into each hole. Dot with ghee.

4 Place a foil round directly on top of the rice. Cover tightly and cook over a low heat for 45–50 minutes. Toss the mixture gently and serve at once.

Lebanese Fish with Rice

INGREDIENTS

juice of 1 lemon
45ml/3 tbsp corn oil
900g/2lb cod steaks
4 large onions, chopped
5ml/1 tsp ground cumin
2–3 saffron strands, soaked in 15ml/1 tbsp
boiling water
1 litre/1¾ pints/4 cups fish stock
450g/1lb/2¼ cups long grain rice
50g/2oz/⅔ cup pine nuts, lightly toasted
salt and ground black pepper
chopped fresh parsley, to garnish

SERVES 4–6

1 Mix the lemon juice with 15ml/1 tbsp of the oil in a shallow dish. Add the fish steaks, turn to coat thoroughly, then cover and marinate for 30 minutes.

2 Heat the remaining oil in a large saucepan. Fry the onions for 5–6 minutes, stirring occasionally. Drain the fish, reserving the marinade, and add the steaks to the pan. Fry for 1–2 minutes on each side, then add the cumin and a little salt and pepper.

3 Strain over the saffron water, then add the fish stock and reserved marinade. Bring to the boil, lower the heat and simmer for 8–10 minutes, until the fish is almost cooked.

4 Using a slotted spoon, transfer the fish steaks to a platter. Add the rice to the stock. Bring to the boil, lower the heat and simmer for 15 minutes.

5 Arrange the fish steaks on top of the rice. Cover tightly and steam for 15–20 minutes over a low heat. Transfer the fish to a plate, then spoon the  rice on to a large flat platter. Arrange the fish on top, sprinkle with the pine nuts and garnish with the chopped fresh parsley. Serve at once.

Smoked Fish Kedgeree

INGREDIENTS

450g / 1lb mixed smoked fish
300ml / ½ pint / 1¼ cups milk
175g / 6oz / scant 1 cup long grain rice
1 lemon slice
50g / 2oz / ¼ cup butter
1 onion, finely chopped
10ml / 2 tsp garam masala
2.5ml / ½ tsp grated nutmeg
15ml / 1 tbsp chopped fresh parsley
salt and ground black pepper
fresh flat leaf parsley and 2 hard-boiled
eggs, halved, to serve

SERVES 6

74

2 Then bring a saucepan of lightly salted water to the boil. Add the rice and the lemon slice and cook for 12 minutes until the rice is just tender. Drain well.

3 Melt the butter in a large heavy-based saucepan. Add the chopped onion and cook until softened, then stir in the rice and fish. Shake the pan to mix the ingredients thoroughly. Toss over the heat for 2 minutes.

4 Stir in the garam masala, grated nutmeg and parsley, and add salt and pepper to taste. Tip the mixture into a warmed dish, garnish with the flat leaf parsley and the hard-boiled eggs and serve at once.

1 Poach the un-cooked smoked fish in the milk for 10 minutes, until it flakes when tested with the tip of a knife. Drain, discarding the milk, and flake the fish.

Place it in a bowl and add any smoked fish that does not require cooking.

Seafood Risotto

INGREDIENTS

60ml/4 tbsp sunflower oil
1 onion, chopped
2 garlic cloves, crushed
225g/8oz/generous 1 cup risotto rice
105ml/7 tbsp white wine
1.5 litres/2½ pints/6 cups hot fish stock
350g/12oz mixed seafood (raw prawns,
mussels, squid rings, clams)
grated rind of ½ lemon
30ml/2 tbsp tomato purée
15ml/1 tbsp chopped fresh parsley
salt and ground black pepper

SERVES 4

2 Add 150ml/¼ pint/⅔ cup of the hot stock. Cook, stirring constantly, until it has been absorbed. Stir in a similar amount of stock until it has been absorbed. Continue in this way until you have added about half the stock.

3 Stir in the mixed seafood and cook over a medium heat for about 2–3 minutes. Add the remaining half of the stock as before, until the rice is creamy and tender.

4 Stir in the lemon rind, tomato purée and the chopped fresh parsley. Season with plenty of salt and ground black pepper. The risotto should be served warm rather than piping hot.

1 Heat the oil in a large heavy-based saucepan and gently cook the onion and garlic for about 4–5 minutes until soft. Add the rice and stir into the contents of the pan, to coat the grains with oil. Pour in the white wine and stir over a medium heat for 2–3 minutes until it has been absorbed.

COOK'S TIP

Heat the fish stock in a saucepan before you start preparing the risotto, and keep it on a low simmer. Adding it in small amounts while stirring is the secret of a smooth, creamy dish.

New Orleans Bacon & Seafood Rice

INGREDIENTS

30ml/2 tbsp corn oil
115g/4oz rindless smoked bacon rashers, diced
1 onion, chopped
2 celery sticks, chopped
2 large garlic cloves, chopped
5ml/1 tsp cayenne pepper
2 bay leaves
5ml/1 tsp dried oregano
2.5ml/½ tsp dried thyme
4 tomatoes, peeled and chopped
150ml/¼ pint/⅔ cup passata (puréed tomatoes)
350g/12oz/1¾ cups long grain rice
475ml/16fl oz/2 cups stock
175g/6oz skinned haddock fillets, cubed
115g/4oz cooked, peeled prawns
salt and ground black pepper
2 spring onions, chopped, to garnish

SERVES 4

1 Preheat the oven to 180°C/350°F/Gas 4. Heat the oil in a flameproof casserole and fry the bacon until crisp. Add the chopped onion and celery and stir until soft and golden brown.

2 Add the chopped garlic, cayenne, dried herbs and chopped tomatoes, with salt and pepper to taste. Stir in the passata, rice and stock. Bring to the boil.

3 Stir the fish cubes into the rice mixture. Cover tightly. Put the casserole in the oven and bake for 20–30 minutes, until the rice is just tender.

4 Stir in the prawns and heat through. Sprinkle with the chopped spring onions and serve at once.

COOK'S TIP

For a special-occasion garnish, add a whole cooked prawn, in the shell, and a spring onion tassel, to each portion.

Spanish Seafood Paella

INGREDIENTS

60ml/4 tbsp olive oil
225g/8oz monkfish, skinned and cubed
3 prepared baby squid, body cut into rings and
tentacles chopped
1 onion, chopped
3 garlic cloves, finely chopped
1 red pepper, seeded and sliced
4 tomatoes, peeled and chopped
225g/8oz/generous 1 cup risotto rice
450ml/3/4 pint/1 3/4 cups fish stock
150ml/1/4 pint/2/3 cup white wine
4–5 saffron strands, soaked in 30ml/2 tbsp
boiling water
75g/3oz/3/4 cup frozen peas
115g/4oz cooked, peeled prawns
8 fresh mussels, scrubbed and debearded
salt and ground black pepper
chopped fresh parsley, to garnish
lemon wedges, to serve

SERVES 4

1 Heat 30ml/2 tbsp of the oil in a paella pan and stir-fry the monkfish cubes with the squid for 2 minutes. Tip into a bowl and set aside.

2 Heat the remaining oil in the clean pan and fry the onion, garlic and pepper until softened. Stir in the tomatoes and rice. Cook for 4 minutes, stirring, then add the fish stock, wine, strained saffron liquid and peas, with salt and pepper to taste.

3 Gently stir in the monkfish, squid and prawns. Push the mussels into the rice. Cover tightly. Cook gently for 30 minutes, until most of the stock has been absorbed and the mussels have opened. (Discard any that remain closed.)

4 Remove the paella from the heat. Leave to stand, covered, for 5 minutes. Sprinkle with the parsley and serve with lemon wedges.

Fried Singapore Noodles

INGREDIENTS

175g/6oz dried rice noodles, soaked in hot
water until soft
60ml/4 tbsp vegetable oil
2.5ml/½ tsp salt
2.5ml/½ tsp sugar
10ml/2 tsp curry powder
75g/3oz cooked prawns, peeled and deveined
175g/6oz cold roast pork, cut into matchsticks
1 green pepper, seeded and chopped
into matchsticks
75g/3oz Thai fish cakes (optional)
10ml/2 tsp dark soy sauce

SERVES 4

81

1 Drain the noodles. Pat them dry with kitchen paper. Heat a wok, then add half the oil. When hot, add the noodles and salt. Toss over the heat for 2 minutes, then use two slotted spoons to drain the noodles and transfer them to a serving dish. Keep hot.

2 Gently heat the remaining oil in the wok. Stir in the sugar and curry powder and fry for 30 seconds. Add the prawns, pork and pepper. Stir-fry for 1 minute.

3 Return the noodles to the wok and add the Thai fish cakes, if you are using them. Stir-fry for 2 minutes more, until heated through. Stir in the soy sauce and serve immediately.

Stir-fried Noodles with Salmon

INGREDIENTS

350g/12oz salmon fillet
3 garlic cloves
30ml/2 tbsp Japanese soy sauce (shoyu)
30ml/2 tbsp sake
60ml/4 tbsp mirin or sweet sherry
5ml/1 tsp soft light brown sugar
10ml/2 tsp grated fresh root ginger
30ml/2 tbsp groundnut oil
225g/8oz dried egg noodles, cooked
and drained
50g/2oz/1 cup alfalfa sprouts
30ml/2 tbsp sesame seeds, lightly toasted,
to garnish

SERVES 4

1 Slice the salmon thinly and spread the slices out in a large shallow dish. Crush 1 garlic clove and slice the remaining garlic thinly. Mix the soy sauce, sake, mirin

or sherry, sugar, ginger and crushed garlic in a jug. Pour the mixture over the salmon slices, cover and marinate for 30 minutes.

2 Carefully drain the salmon slices, reserving the marinade. Scrape any remaining pieces of ginger or garlic off the fish, then arrange the salmon slices in a

single layer in a large ovenproof dish and set aside. Pre-heat the grill.

3 Heat a wok, add the oil and swirl it around. Cook the sliced garlic until it is golden brown, then add the cooked noodles and reserved marinade. Stir-fry for

3–4 minutes, until the marinade has reduced to a syrupy glaze that coats the noodles.

4 Meanwhile, cook the salmon slices under the hot grill for 2–3 minutes without turning. When the salmon is tender, toss the alfalfa sprouts with the noodle mixture and arrange on four individual heated plates. Top the noodle mixture with the salmon slices and sprinkle the toasted sesame seeds over the top. Serve at once.

82

Seafood Chow Mein

INGREDIENTS

*75g/3oz squid, cleaned (see Chilli Squid
with Noodles)*
½ egg white
*15ml/1 tbsp cornflour, mixed to a
paste with water*
*75g/3oz raw prawns, peeled, deveined and
cut in half lengthways*
3–4 fresh scallops, each cut into 3–4 slices
250g/9oz dried egg noodles
75–90ml/5–6 tbsp vegetable oil
50g/2oz mangetouts, trimmed
2.5ml/½ tsp salt
2.5ml/½ tsp soft light brown sugar
15ml/1 tbsp rice wine or dry sherry
30ml/2 tbsp soy sauce
2 spring onions, finely sliced
vegetable stock to moisten (optional)
few drops of sesame oil

SERVES 4

1 Open up the body of the squid and score the inner flesh in a criss-cross pattern. Cut it into tiny pieces, each about the size of a stamp. Add them to a bowl of boiling water and leave until all of them have curled up. Rinse under cold water and drain.

2 Whisk the egg white and cornflour paste in a bowl, add the prawns and scallops and stir to coat. Bring a saucepan of lightly salted water to the boil and cook the noodles. Drain, rinse under cold water and drain again. Tip into a bowl and toss with 15ml/1 tbsp of the oil.

3 Heat 30–45ml/2–3 tbsp oil in a wok. Stir-fry the mangetouts and seafood for 2 minutes. Add the salt, sugar and the wine or sherry, then stir in half the soy sauce. Add half the spring onions and moisten with a little stock if necessary. Toss over the heat for 1 minute, then remove and keep hot.

4 Heat the remaining oil in the wok. Stir-fry the noodles with the remaining soy sauce for 2–3 minutes. Place in a serving dish and mix in the seafood mixture. Garnish with the remaining spring onions and drizzle with the sesame oil. Serve hot or cold.

Lemon Grass Prawns

INGREDIENTS

300g/11oz thin dried egg noodles, cooked
and drained
60ml/4 tbsp vegetable oil
500g/1¼lb raw king prawns, peeled
and deveined
2.5ml/½ tsp ground coriander
15ml/1 tbsp ground turmeric
2 garlic cloves, finely chopped
2 slices of fresh root ginger, peeled and
finely chopped
2 lemon grass stalks, finely chopped
2 shallots, finely chopped
15ml/1 tbsp tomato purée
250ml/8fl oz/1 cup coconut cream
15–30ml/1–2 tbsp fresh lime juice
15–30ml/1–2 tbsp fish sauce
1 cucumber, peeled, seeded and cut into
5cm/2in batons
1 tomato, peeled, seeded and cut into strips
2 fresh red chillies, seeded and thinly sliced
salt and ground black pepper
spring onions and fresh coriander, to garnish

SERVES 4

2 Put the prawns, ground spices, garlic, ginger and lemon grass in a bowl. Add salt and pepper to taste and toss to coat. Heat the remaining oil in a large frying pan and stir-fry the shallots for 1 minute, then add the seasoned prawns and stir-fry for 2 minutes. Remove the prawns with a slotted spoon.

3 Stir the tomato purée and coconut cream into the mixture remaining in the pan. Add lime juice and fish sauce to taste. Bring to simmering point, then add the cucumber. Return the prawns to the sauce and simmer for 3–4 minutes, until they are tender and the sauce is thick.

1 Fry the noodles in 15ml/1 tbsp of the oil as described for Pork Satay with Crisp Noodle Cake (page 55), to make four individual cakes. Keep hot.

4 Add the tomato, stir until heated, then add the chillies. Serve on the noodle cakes, garnished with sliced spring onions and fresh coriander sprigs.

Spicy Fried Rice Sticks

INGREDIENTS

15g/½oz dried shrimps, soaked in hot water
for 30 minutes
225g/8oz dried rice sticks, soaked in hot water
for 30 minutes
30ml/2 tbsp tamarind water
45ml/3 tbsp fish sauce
15ml/1 tbsp granulated sugar
2 garlic cloves, chopped
2 fresh red chillies, seeded and chopped
45ml/3 tbsp groundnut oil
2 eggs, beaten
225g/8oz cooked king prawns, peeled
and deveined
3 spring onions, cut into 2.5cm/1in lengths
75g/3oz/1½ cups beansprouts
30ml/2 tbsp chopped roasted unsalted peanuts
30ml/2 tbsp chopped fresh coriander
lime slices, to garnish

SERVES 4

1 Drain the shrimps and set them aside. Drain the rice sticks, rinse them under cold running water and drain again. Mix the tamarind water with the fish sauce and sugar.

2 Put the garlic and chillies in a mortar and use a pestle to pound them to a paste. Heat a wok, add 15ml/1 tbsp of the oil, then stir-fry the eggs over a medium heat until lightly scrambled. Transfer the eggs to a bowl and set aside. Wipe the wok clean.

3 Reheat the wok, add the remaining oil, then fry the chilli and garlic paste with the dried shrimps for 1 minute. Add the rice sticks and tamarind mixture; toss over the heat for 3–4 minutes.

4 Add the scrambled eggs, prawns, spring onions, beansprouts, peanuts and coriander to the wok. Toss over the heat for 2 minutes until heated through and well mixed. Serve at once on individual plates, garnishing each portion with lime slices.

COOK'S TIP

For a vegetarian dish, leave out the dried
shrimps and use cubes of deep-fried, plain
or smoked, firm tofu instead of the prawns.

VEGETABLES, VEGETARIAN AND SALADS

Broccoli Risotto Torte

INGREDIENTS

225g/8oz broccoli, cut into tiny florets
50g/2oz/4 tbsp butter
30ml/2 tbsp olive oil, plus extra for greasing
1 onion, chopped
2 garlic cloves, crushed
1 large yellow pepper, seeded and sliced
225g/8oz/generous 1 cup risotto rice
120ml/4fl oz/½ cup dry white wine
1 litre/1¾ pints/4 cups vegetable stock
115g/4oz/1⅓ cups grated Parmesan cheese
4 eggs, separated
salt and ground black pepper
tomato slices and chopped parsley, to garnish

SERVES 4

1 Blanch the broccoli in boiling water for 3 minutes, drain and set aside. Melt the butter in the oil in a frying pan. Fry the onion, garlic and pepper until soft.

2 Stir in the rice, cook for 1 minute, then pour in the wine. Cook, stirring constantly, until it is absorbed. Pour in the stock and season well. Bring to the boil, lower the heat and simmer for 20 minutes, stirring occasionally.

3 Preheat the oven to 180°C/350°F/Gas 4. Lightly grease a deep 25cm/10in round cake tin and base line it with non-stick baking paper. Stir the cheese into the rice mixture, cool for 5 minutes, then beat in the egg yolks. Fold in the broccoli.

4 Whisk the egg whites to stiff peaks; fold them into the rice. Spoon into the prepared tin and bake for 1 hour, until risen, golden and still slightly wobbly in the centre. Cool slightly, then invert on a serving plate and peel off the paper and turn back on to a serving plate. Garnish with tomato slices and parsley. This torte is also good served cold.

Risotto alla Milanese

INGREDIENTS

25g/1oz/2 tbsp butter
1 large onion, finely chopped
275g/10oz/1½ cups risotto rice
150ml/¼ pint/⅔ cup dry white wine
5ml/1 tsp saffron strands soaked in
15ml/1 tbsp boiling water
1 litre/1¾ pints/4 cups vegetable stock
salt and ground black pepper
Parmesan cheese shavings, to garnish
GREMOLATA
2 garlic cloves, crushed
60ml/4 tbsp chopped fresh parsley
finely grated rind of 1 lemon

SERVES 4

1 Make the gremolata by mixing the garlic and parsley in a bowl. Stir in the grated lemon rind and set aside.

2 Melt the butter in a heavy-based saucepan. Add the onion and fry over a low heat for 5 minutes. Stir in the rice until well coated. Cook for 2 minutes, until it is translucent, then add the wine and strain in the saffron liquid. Cook for 3–4 minutes, until the liquid has been absorbed.

3 Add 600ml/1 pint/2½ cups of the stock to the saucepan. Simmer, stirring frequently, until it has been absorbed. Gradually add the remaining stock, a ladleful at a time, until the rice is tender and creamy. Allow each quantity of stock to be absorbed before adding the next (it may not be necessary to add it all).

4 Season the risotto with plenty of salt and pepper. Transfer it to a serving dish. Scatter lavishly with the Parmesan shavings and gremolata. Serve hot.

91

Mexican-style Rice

Ingredients

350g/12oz/1¾ cups long grain white rice
1 onion, chopped
2 garlic cloves, chopped
450g/1lb tomatoes, peeled, seeded and
coarsely chopped
60ml/4 tbsp corn or peanut oil
900ml/1½ pints/3¾ cups chicken stock
4–6 small red chillies
175g/6oz/1 cup cooked green peas
salt and ground black pepper
fresh coriander springs, to garnish

Serves 6

1 First soak the rice in a bowl of hot water for 15 minutes. Drain, rinse well under cold running water, drain again and set aside.

2 Combine the onion, garlic and tomatoes in a food processor and process to a purée.

3 Heat the oil in a large frying pan or wok. Add the drained rice and sauté until it is golden brown. Using a slotted spoon, transfer the rice to a saucepan.

4 Reheat the oil remaining in the pan and cook the tomato purée for 2–3 minutes. Tip it in the saucepan, pour in the stock and season to taste.

5 Bring to the boil, reduce the heat to the lowest setting, cover the pan and cook for 15–20 minutes until almost all the liquid is absorbed. Slice the red chillies from tip to stem end into four or five sections. Place in a bowl of iced water until they curl back to form flowers, then drain.

6 Stir the peas into the rice mixture and cook, without a lid, until the liquid is absorbed and the rice tender. Stir the mixture occasionally.

7 Transfer the rice to a serving dish and garnish with the drained chilli flowers and coriander sprigs. Warn your guests that these exotic chilli "flowers" are hot and should be approached with caution.

Parsnip, Aubergine & Cashew Biryani

INGREDIENTS

1 small aubergine, sliced
3 onions
2 garlic cloves
2.5cm / 1in piece of fresh root ginger, roughly chopped
45ml / 3 tbsp water
60ml / 4 tbsp corn oil
175g / 6oz / 1½ cups unsalted cashew nuts
40g / 1½oz / ¼ cup sultanas
1 red pepper, seeded and sliced
3 parsnips, roughly chopped
5ml / 1 tsp ground cumin
5ml / 1 tsp ground coriander
2.5ml / ½ tsp chilli powder
120ml / 4fl oz / ½ cup natural yogurt
120ml / 4fl oz / ½ cup vegetable stock
275g / 10oz / 1⅓ cups basmati rice, soaked
25g / 1oz / 2 tbsp butter
salt and ground black pepper
fresh coriander sprigs and quartered hard-boiled eggs, to garnish

SERVES 4–6

1 Sprinkle the aubergine slices with salt and leave to drain for 30 minutes. Rinse the slices, pat dry and cut into bite-size pieces. Chop 1 onion roughly and place it in a food processor with the garlic and ginger. Add the water and process to a paste.

2 Slice the remaining onions finely. Heat 45ml/ 3 tbsp of the oil in a pan and fry the onions until golden. Drain well and place in a bowl. Stir-fry the cashews in the oil for 2 minutes, then add the sultanas and fry until they swell. Using a slotted spoon, transfer to the onions in the bowl. Stir-fry the aubergine, pepper and parsnips for 5 minutes, then lift out with a slotted spoon and set aside.

3 Heat the remaining oil and cook the onion paste until golden. Stir in the spices and cook for 1 minute, then lower the heat and stir in the yogurt, stock and aubergine mixture. Bring to the boil, lower the heat and simmer for 30 minutes. Tip the mixture into a baking dish and set aside.

4 Cook the drained rice in salted boiling water for 5 minutes, until tender but undercooked. Drain and mound on top of the vegetable mixture. Push a long spoon handle through the mixture and scatter the reserved onion mixture evenly on top. Dot with butter and cover with foil and a tight-fitting lid.

5 Bake the biryani for 35–40 minutes, then spoon on to a heated serving dish. Garnish with the fresh coriander and hard-boiled eggs and serve.

Wild Rice with Grilled Vegetables

INGREDIENTS

75g/3oz/scant ½ cup wild rice
150g/5oz/⅔ cup long grain rice
1 large aubergine, thickly sliced
1 each red, yellow and green peppers, seeded and sliced
2 red onions, sliced
225g/8oz/2 cups brown cap or shiitake mushrooms
2 small courgettes, cut in half lengthways
olive oil, for brushing
30ml/2 tbsp chopped fresh thyme
DRESSING
90ml/6 tbsp extra virgin olive oil
30ml/2 tbsp balsamic vinegar
2 garlic cloves, crushed
salt and ground black pepper

SERVES 4

1 Put both types of rice in a pan of water and add salt. Bring to the boil, then lower the heat, cover and cook for 30–40 minutes or until the rice is tender.

2 Meanwhile, make the dressing and grill the vegetables. Mix the olive oil, vinegar and garlic in a screw-top jar. Add salt and pepper to taste, close the lid tightly and shake until thoroughly blended.

3 Arrange the aubergine, peppers, onions, mushrooms and courgettes on a grill rack. Brush with the olive oil and cook under a hot grill for 8–10 minutes until well browned. Turn the vegetables occasionally and brush with oil.

4 Drain the rice mixture and tip it into a bowl. Shake the dressing again, pour half of it over the rice and mix. Spoon into a large serving dish and arrange the grilled vegetables on top. Drizzle the remaining dressing over and garnish with the thyme.

COOK'S TIP

Grilled vegetables taste and look wonderful when cooked on the barbecue. Use a solid ridged grill if you have one, to save slices from falling on to the coals.

96

Persian Rice & Lentils

INGREDIENTS

450g / 1lb / 2¼ cups basmati rice, soaked
150ml / ¼ pint / ⅔ cup oil
2 onions, 1 chopped and 1 thinly sliced
2 garlic cloves, crushed
150g / 5oz / ⅔ cup green lentils, soaked and drained
600ml / 1 pint / 2½ cups vegetable stock
50g / 2oz / ⅓ cup raisins
10ml / 2 tsp ground coriander
45ml / 3 tbsp tomato purée
1 egg yolk, beaten
10ml / 2 tsp natural yogurt
75g / 3oz / 6 tbsp ghee, melted
few saffron strands soaked in 10ml / 2 tsp boiling water
salt and ground black pepper
fresh herbs, to garnish

SERVES 8

1 Cook the drained rice in lightly salted boiling water for 3 minutes only. Drain well.

2 Heat 30ml/2 tbsp of the oil in a deep saucepan and fry the chopped onion and garlic for 5 minutes. Stir in the lentils, stock, raisins, coriander, tomato purée, and salt and pepper to taste. Bring to the boil, lower the heat, cover and simmer for 20 minutes.

3 Meanwhile, spoon 115g/4oz/1 cup of the cooked rice into a bowl and stir in the egg yolk and yogurt. Add plenty of salt and pepper. Mix well.

4 Heat two-thirds of the remaining oil in a pan. Spread the yogurt-flavoured rice over the base. Layer the plain rice and the lentil mixture in the pan, ending with the plain rice.

5 With a spoon handle, make three holes down to the bottom of the pan. Drizzle over the ghee. Bring to a high heat, then wrap the pan lid in a clean, wet dish towel and fit on top. When steam appears, lower the heat and simmer for 30 minutes. Fry the sliced onion until browned. Drain well.

6 Keeping the lid on, stand the pan of rice in cold water to loosen the golden crust on the bottom. Scoop about 60ml/4 tbsp of the plain rice into a bowl, strain over the saffron water and mix lightly.

7 Toss the rice and lentil mixture and mound it on a platter. Scatter the saffron rice on top. Break up the rice crust on the bottom of the pan and place it around the mound. Scatter the fried onion over, garnish with fresh herbs and serve.

Nutty Rice & Mushroom Stir-fry

INGREDIENTS

45ml/3 tbsp sunflower oil
450g/1lb/4 cups cooked long grain rice
1 small onion, roughly chopped
225g/8oz/2 cups field mushrooms, sliced
50g/2oz/½ cup hazelnuts, roughly chopped
50g/2oz/½ cup pecan nuts, roughly chopped
50g/2oz/½ cup blanched almonds, roughly
chopped
60ml/4 tbsp chopped fresh parsley
salt and ground black pepper

SERVES 4–6

1 Heat half the oil in a wok. Add the rice and stir-fry for 2–3 minutes over a moderately high heat. Remove the rice from the wok and set aside. Then heat the remaining

oil in the wok and stir-fry the chopped onion for 2 minutes, until softened.

2 Stir the sliced mushrooms into the wok with the onion. Toss over the heat for 2 minutes more.

3 Add all the nuts to the wok and stir-fry for 1 minute. Return the rice to the wok and stir-fry for 3 minutes. Add plenty of salt and pepper to taste. Stir in the chopped fresh parsley and serve at once.

COOK'S TIP

This is a wonderful way of using up leftover rice. Try brown rice, as a variation, and add cashews instead of almonds.

Festive Rice

INGREDIENTS

450g / 1lb / 2¼ cups Thai fragrant rice
60ml / 4 tbsp oil
2 garlic cloves, crushed
2 onions, finely sliced
5cm / 2in piece of fresh turmeric, peeled and crushed
750ml / 1¼ pints / 3 cups water
350ml / 12fl oz / 1½ cups coconut milk
1–2 lemon grass stems, bruised
ACCOMPANIMENTS
omelette strips
2 fresh chillies, shredded
cucumber chunks
tomato wedges
deep-fried onions
prawn crackers

SERVES 8

1 Wash the rice in several changes of water. Drain well. Heat the oil in a wok and gently fry the garlic, onions and turmeric for 3–4 minutes, until the onions have softened, but not browned.

2 Stir in the rice until coated, then pour in the water and coconut milk. Add the lemon grass. Bring to the boil, lower the heat and simmer for 15 minutes, until all the liquid has been absorbed.

3 Remove the pan from the heat, cover with a clean dish towel and a tight-fitting lid and leave to stand in a warm place for 15 minutes.

4 Lift out the lemon grass and discard. Spread the rice mixture on a platter and garnish with the accompaniments. Serve at once.

Green Lentil Filo Pie

INGREDIENTS

175g/6oz/1 cup green lentils, soaked for
30 minutes in water to cover, drained
2 bay leaves
2 onions, sliced
1.2 litres/2 pints/5 cups stock
175g/6oz/¾ cup butter, melted
225g/8oz/1¼ cups long grain rice,
ideally basmati
60ml/4 tbsp chopped fresh parsley, plus a few
sprigs to garnish
30ml/2 tbsp chopped fresh dill
1 egg, beaten
225g/8oz/2 cups mushrooms, sliced
about 8 sheets filo pastry
3 eggs, hard-boiled and sliced
salt and ground black pepper

SERVES 6

I Cover the lentils with water, then simmer with the bay leaves, one onion and half the stock for 20–25 minutes, or until tender. Season well. Set aside to cool.

2 Gently fry the remaining onion in another saucepan in 25g/1oz/2 tbsp of the butter, for 5 minutes. Stir in the rice and the rest of the stock. Season, bring to the boil, then cover and simmer for 12 minutes for basmati, 15 minutes for long grain. Leave to stand, uncovered, for 5 minutes, then stir in the fresh herbs and the beaten egg.

3 Fry the mushrooms in 45ml/3 tbsp of the butter for 5 minutes, until they are just soft. Set aside to cool. Preheat the oven to 190°C/375°F/Gas 5.

4 Brush the inside of a large, shallow ovenproof dish with more butter. Lay the sheets of filo in it, covering the base but making sure most of the filo hangs over the sides. Brush the sheets of filo well with butter as you go and overlap the pastry as required. Ensure there is a lot of pastry to fold over the mounded green lentil filling.

5 Into the pastry lining, layer rice, lentils and mushrooms, repeating the layers at least once and tucking the sliced egg in between. Season as you layer and form an even mound of filling. Bring up the sheets of pastry over the filling, scrunching the top into attractive folds. Brush all over with the rest of the butter and set aside to chill and firm up.

6 Bake the pie for about 45 minutes, until golden and crisp. Allow it to stand for 10 minutes before serving, garnished with parsley.

102

Tomato Rice

INGREDIENTS

30ml / 2 tbsp corn oil
2.5ml / ½ tsp onion seeds
1 onion, sliced
2 tomatoes, sliced
1 orange or yellow pepper, seeded, roughly
chopped and cut into chunks
5ml / 1 tsp grated fresh root ginger
1 garlic clove, crushed
5ml / 1 tsp chilli powder
30ml / 2 tbsp chopped fresh coriander
1 potato, diced
7.5ml / 1½ tsp salt
50g / 2oz / scant ½ cup frozen peas
400g / 14oz / 2 cups basmati rice, soaked
750ml / 1¼ pints / 3 cups water

SERVES 4

104

2 Add the sliced tomatoes, pepper, ginger, garlic, chilli powder, fresh coriander, diced potato, salt and peas. Stir-fry over a medium heat for 5 minutes more.

3 Stir in the drained rice until well coated. Pour the water over and bring to the boil, then lower the heat slightly, cover tightly and cook for 12–15 minutes. Remove the rice from the heat, leaving the lid in place, and set aside for 5 minutes. Tip into a warmed serving dish, fork up the rice and serve.

1 Heat the oil in a large saucepan and fry the onion seeds for about 30 seconds. Add the sliced onion and fry for 5 minutes more until they are lightly toasted.

Tofu Noodles

Ingredients

225g/8oz firm tofu
groundnut oil, for deep-frying
175g/6oz dried medium egg noodles
15ml/1 tbsp sesame oil
5ml/1 tsp cornflour
10ml/2 tsp dark soy sauce
30ml/2 tbsp rice wine or dry sherry
5ml/1 tsp granulated sugar
6–8 spring onions, cut diagonally
into 2.5cm/1in lengths
3 garlic cloves, sliced
1 fresh green chilli, seeded and sliced
115g/4oz Chinese cabbage leaves,
coarsely shredded
50g/2oz/1 cup beansprouts
50g/2oz/½ cup cashew nuts, toasted, to serve

Serves 4

1 Drain the tofu, pat it dry with kitchen paper and cut into 2.5cm/1in cubes. Half-fill a wok with groundnut oil and heat it to 180°C/350°F or until a cube of dried bread added to the oil browns in 30–45 seconds. Deep-fry the tofu in batches for 1–2 minutes or until golden brown. Drain on kitchen paper. Carefully pour all but 30ml/2 tbsp of the oil from the wok.

2 Bring a saucepan of lightly salted water to the boil. Add the noodles and cook according to the instructions on the packet. Drain, rinse under cold water and drain again. Tip into a bowl and toss with 10ml/2 tsp of the sesame oil. Mix the cornflour, soy sauce, rice wine or sherry, sugar and remaining sesame oil in a small bowl.

3 Reheat the oil in the wok and stir-fry the spring onions, garlic, chilli, Chinese cabbage and beansprouts for 1–2 minutes. Toss in the tofu and noodles, then add the cornflour mixture. Cook, stirring, for 1 minute. Sprinkle with the toasted cashews and serve.

Crispy Noodles with Mixed Vegetables

INGREDIENTS

2 large carrots
2 courgettes
4 spring onions
115g/4oz fine green beans
115g/4oz dried rice vermicelli or
cellophane noodles
groundnut oil, for deep-frying
2.5cm/1in piece of fresh root ginger, peeled and
cut into shreds
1 fresh red chilli, sliced
115g/4oz/1 cup fresh shiitake or button
mushrooms, thickly sliced
a few Chinese cabbage leaves, coarsely shredded
75g/3oz/1½ cups beansprouts
30ml/2 tbsp light soy sauce
30ml/2 tbsp rice wine or dry sherry
5ml/1 tsp granulated sugar
30ml/2 tbsp torn fresh coriander leaves

SERVES 3–4

1 Cut the carrots, courgettes and spring onions into matchsticks. Trim the beans. Break the vermicelli or noodles into 7.5cm/3in lengths.

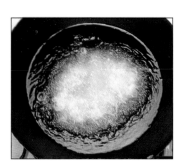

2 Half-fill a wok with groundnut oil and heat it to 180°C/350°F or until a cube of dried bread added to the oil browns in 30–45 seconds. Deep-fry the dried vermicelli or noodles, a handful at a time, for 1–2 minutes, until puffed up and crisp. Drain on kitchen paper. Carefully pour away all but 30ml/2 tbsp of the oil from the wok.

3 Reheat the oil in the wok and stir-fry the beans and carrots for 2–3 minutes. Add the ginger, chilli, mushrooms and courgettes and stir-fry for 1–2 minutes more.

4 Add the Chinese cabbage, beansprouts and spring onions and stir-fry for 1 minute more. Spoon over the soy sauce, rice wine or sherry and sugar. Toss over the heat for 30 seconds, then add the vermicelli or noodles and the fresh coriander. Toss to mix, taking care not to crush the noodles, then serve.

Sesame Noodle Salad with Hot Peanuts

INGREDIENTS

350g/12oz dried egg noodles
2 carrots, cut into matchsticks
½ cucumber, peeled and cubed
115g/4oz celeriac, cut into matchsticks
6 spring onions, finely sliced
8 canned water chestnuts, drained and finely sliced
175g/6oz/3 cups beansprouts
1 fresh green chilli, seeded and finely chopped
30ml/2 tbsp sesame seeds and
115g/4oz peanuts, to serve
DRESSING
15ml/1 tbsp dark soy sauce
15ml/1 tbsp light soy sauce
15ml/1 tbsp clear honey
15ml/1 tbsp rice wine or dry sherry
15ml/1 tbsp sesame oil

SERVES 4

1 Preheat the oven to 200°C/400°F/Gas 6. Bring a saucepan of lightly salted water to the boil. Add the noodles and cook according to the instructions on the packet. Drain the noodles, rinse under cold water and drain again.

2 Tip the noodles into a bowl and add the prepared vegetables, including the chilli. Mix well. Combine the dressing ingredients in a small bowl, whisk lightly, then add to the salad and toss to coat. Divide the salad between four plates.

3 Spread out the sesame seeds and peanuts on separate baking sheets. Bake the sesame seeds for 5 minutes and the peanuts for 10 minutes or until evenly browned.

4 Sprinkle the roasted seeds and peanuts over the four plates of salad and serve.

Stir-fried Vegetables with Ribbon Noodles

Ingredients

*450g/1lb dried ribbon noodles,
such as tagliatelle
45ml/3 tbsp corn oil
1cm/½in piece of fresh root ginger, peeled
and finely chopped
2 garlic cloves, crushed
1 carrot, sliced diagonally
2 courgettes, quartered lengthways,
then sliced diagonally
175g/6oz runner beans, sliced diagonally
175g/6oz baby corn cobs, halved lengthways
90ml/6 tbsp yellow bean sauce
6 spring onions, sliced into 2.5cm/1in lengths
30ml/2 tbsp rice wine or dry sherry
5ml/1 tsp sesame seeds
salt*

SERVES 4

1 Bring a large saucepan of lightly salted water to the boil. Cook the ribbon noodles according to the instructions on the packet. Drain, rinse under hot water and drain again. Tip into a bowl and toss with 5ml/1 tsp of the oil.

2 Heat the rest of the oil in a wok or frying pan and stir-fry the ginger and garlic for 30 seconds, then add the vegetables. Stir-fry for 3–4 minutes.

3 Stir in the yellow bean sauce. Toss over the heat for 2 minutes, then add the spring onions, rice wine or sherry and drained ribbon noodles. Season with salt to taste.

Toss over the heat for 1 minute to heat through. Sprinkle with the sesame seeds and serve at once.

109

Noodles with Shiitake & Red Onion

INGREDIENTS

500g/ 1¼lb thin dried tagliarini
45ml/ 3 tbsp sesame oil
1 red onion, thinly sliced
115g/ 4oz fresh shiitake mushrooms, trimmed
and thinly sliced
45ml/ 3 tbsp dark soy sauce
15ml/ 1 tbsp balsamic vinegar
10ml/ 2 tsp caster sugar
5ml/ 1 tsp salt
celery leaves, to garnish

SERVES 6

3 Add the noodles to the wok, with the soy sauce, balsamic vinegar, caster sugar and salt. Stir-fry for 1 minute more, then add the remaining sesame oil. Toss

over the heat for 30 seconds. Garnish with celery leaves and serve at once.

1 Bring a large saucepan of lightly salted water to the boil. Add the noodles and cook according to the instructions on the packet. Drain, rinse under hot

water and drain again. Tip into a bowl and toss with 5ml/ 1 tsp of the oil.

2 Meanwhile, heat a wok, add 15ml/ 1 tbsp of the remaining oil and stir-fry the onion and shiitake mushrooms for 2 minutes.

Courgettes with Noodle Needles

Ingredients

450g/1lb courgettes
30ml/2 tbsp vegetable oil
1 onion, thinly sliced
1 garlic clove, crushed
2.5ml/½ tsp ground turmeric
2 tomatoes, chopped
45ml/3 tbsp water
400g/14oz cooked prawns, peeled and deveined
25g/1oz cellophane noodles
salt or soy sauce

SERVES 4–6

1 Use a vegetable peeler to cut thin strips from the outside of each courgette. Cut the courgettes into thin slices. The slices will have decorative edges.

2 Heat the oil in a frying pan or wok and fry the onion and garlic for 5 minutes, until softened but not browned. Stir in the courgette slices and ground turmeric, then add the chopped tomatoes, water and prawns.

3 Put the noodles in a saucepan and pour over boiling water to cover. Leave for 1–2 minutes, then drain. Snip into 5cm/2in "needles" and add to the vegetables.

4 Cover with a lid and cook the noodles and vegetables in their own steam for 2–3 minutes. Toss well, season to taste with salt or soy sauce and serve at once.

111

Thai Noodle Salad

INGREDIENTS

350g/12oz dried somen noodles
1 large carrot, cut into thin strips
1 bunch asparagus, trimmed and cut into
4cm/1½in lengths
115g/4oz mangetouts, topped,
tailed and halved
115g/4oz baby corn cobs, halved lengthways
1 red pepper, seeded and cut into fine strips
115g/4oz/2 cups beansprouts
8 canned water chestnuts, drained and
thinly sliced
lime wedges, chopped roasted peanuts and
fresh coriander leaves, to garnish
DRESSING
45ml/3 tbsp torn fresh basil leaves
75ml/5 tbsp roughly chopped mint leaves
2 spring onions, thinly sliced
15ml/1 tbsp grated fresh root ginger
2 garlic cloves, crushed
250ml/8fl oz/1 cup coconut milk
30ml/2 tbsp dark sesame oil
juice of 1 lime
salt and cayenne pepper

SERVES 4–6

1 Make the dressing. Combine the fresh herb leaves and spring onions in a bowl. Add the ginger and garlic, coconut milk, sesame oil and lime juice. Whisk well, then season to taste with the salt and cayenne.

2 Bring a saucepan of lightly salted water to the boil. Add the noodles and cook according to the instructions on the packet. Drain, rinse under cold water and drain again.

3 Cook the carrot, asparagus, mangetouts and corn in separate saucepans of lightly salted boiling water until crisp-tender. Drain, refresh under cold water and drain again. Tip into a bowl and add the red pepper, beansprouts and water chestnuts.

4 Add the noodles and dressing to the bowl and toss well. Arrange on individual plates and garnish with the lime wedges, peanuts and coriander leaves.

Fruit & Vegetable Gado-Gado

INGREDIENTS

½ cucumber, sliced
2 pears, not too ripe
1–2 eating apples
30ml/2 tbsp lemon juice
1 small crisp lettuce, shredded
6 small tomatoes, cut into wedges
3 fresh pineapple slices, cored and
cut into wedges
12 hard-boiled quail's eggs, shelled
175g/6oz dried egg noodles, cooked, rinsed,
drained and cut into short lengths
salt
deep fried onions, to garnish
PEANUT SAUCE
15ml/1 tbsp sambal oelek or chilli sauce
300ml/½ pint/1¼ cups coconut milk
350g/12oz/1 cup crunchy peanut butter
15ml/1 tbsp dark soy sauce
10ml/2 tsp thick tamarind water
15ml/1 tbsp peanuts, coarsely crushed
salt

SERVES 6

114

1 Put the cucumber slices in a colander and sprinkle them with salt. Leave in the sink for 15 minutes to drain, then rinse thoroughly and drain again.

2 Then make the peanut sauce. Mix the sambal oelek or chilli sauce with the coconut milk in a saucepan. Add the peanut butter and heat gently, stirring, until the sauce is smooth and thick. Stir in the soy sauce and tamarind water. Pour the sauce into a bowl and sprinkle with the crushed peanuts to serve.

3 Peel the pears and the apples, remove the cores and slice thinly into a bowl. Toss with the lemon juice. Arrange the fruit slices on a platter with the shredded lettuce, cucumber slices, tomatoes and pineapple wedges.

4 Arrange the quail's eggs over the salad and add the chopped noodles and deep fried onions. Serve with the peanut sauce.

PUDDINGS
AND DESSERTS

Caramel Rice Pudding

INGREDIENTS

50g/2oz/5 tbsp short grain pudding rice
75ml/5 tbsp demerara sugar
400g/14oz can evaporated milk, made up to
600ml/1 pint/2½ cups with water
knob of butter
2 crisp eating apples
1 small fresh pineapple
10ml/2 tsp lemon juice

SERVES 4

1 Preheat the oven to 150°C/300°F/Gas 2. Lightly grease a soufflé dish. Put the rice in a sieve and wash thoroughly under cold water. Drain well and tip into the soufflé dish.

2 Add 30ml/2 tbsp of the demerara sugar to the dish. Pour on the diluted evaporated milk and stir. Dot the surface with butter. Bake for 2 hours, then leave to cool for 30 minutes.

3 Meanwhile, core and slice the apples. Peel and core the pineapple and cut it into chunks. Put the fruit in a bowl. Add the lemon juice and toss lightly. Preheat the grill to the maximum heat.

4 Sprinkle the remaining sugar over the baked pudding. Grill until the sugar has caramelized. Leave to stand for 5 minutes, to allow the caramel topping to harden, then serve with the fresh fruit.

Souffléed Rice Pudding

INGREDIENTS

*65g / 2½oz / 5 tbsp short grain pudding
rice, rinsed
45ml / 3 tbsp clear honey
750ml / 1¼ pints / 3 cups milk
2.5ml / ½ tsp vanilla essence
2 egg whites
5ml / 1 tsp grated nutmeg*

SERVES 4

3 Whisk the egg whites in a clean, dry bowl until soft peaks form. Using a large metal spoon, fold them lightly and evenly into the rice mixture. Tip the mixture into the prepared dish and level the surface.

4 Sprinkle with grated nutmeg and bake in the oven for 15–20 minutes, until the pudding is well risen and golden brown. Serve hot.

1 Place the rice, honey and milk in a heavy-based saucepan. Bring to just below boiling point, then simmer over the lowest possible heat for 1–1¼ hours, stirring occasionally, until most of the liquid has been absorbed.

2 Preheat the oven to 220°C/425°F/Gas 7. Lightly grease a 1 litre/1¾ pint/4 cup ovenproof dish. Away from the heat, stir the vanilla essence into the rice mixture and set the saucepan aside to cool slightly.

Moroccan Rice Pudding

INGREDIENTS

25g/1oz/¼ cup blanched almonds, chopped
450ml/¾ pint/1¾ cups very hot water
150g/5oz/¾ cup short grain pudding
rice, rinsed
25g/1oz/2 tbsp butter
7.5cm/3in piece of cinnamon stick
pinch of salt
2.5ml/½ tsp almond essence
400g/14oz can condensed milk, made
up to 600ml/1 pint/2½ cups with
semi-skimmed milk
30ml/2 tbsp orange flower water
toasted flaked almonds and ground cinnamon,
to decorate

SERVES 6

120

1 Process the almonds in a blender or food processor until very fine, then add 120ml/4fl oz/ ½ cup of the hot water and process again. Strain through a sieve into a large saucepan, pressing the nut pulp against the mesh with a spoon to extract as much liquid as possible.

2 Stir the remaining hot water into the almond "milk" and bring to the boil. Add the rice and half the butter to the pan, then add the cinnamon stick. Stir in the salt and almond essence. Pour in half the diluted condensed milk mixture and stir well.

3 Bring to the boil, stirring constantly, then simmer over the lowest possible heat for 1–1½ hours, stirring in the remaining milk mixture towards the end of the cooking time, until the pudding is thick and creamy. Stir in the orange flower water.

4 Pour the rice pudding into a warmed serving bowl, sprinkle with the flaked almonds and dot with the remaining butter. Dust the ground cinnamon over the top and serve.

COOK'S TIP
This is delicious with a topping of Greek-style yogurt and a drizzle of clear honey. Use a delicately scented honey, such as orange blossom.

Fruited Rice Ring

INGREDIENTS

*65g / 2½oz / 5 tbsp short grain pudding
rice, rinsed
900ml / 1½ pints / 3¾ cups milk
5cm / 2in piece of cinnamon stick
175g / 6oz / 1 cup dried fruit salad
175ml / 6fl oz / ¾ cup orange juice
oil, for brushing
45ml / 3 tbsp caster sugar
thinly grated rind of 1 small orange
whipped cream, to serve (optional)*

SERVES 4

122

1 Place the rice, milk and cinnamon stick in a large saucepan. Bring to the boil, then simmer over the lowest possible heat for about 1½ hours, stirring occasion-

ally, until all the liquid has been absorbed.

2 Meanwhile, mix the dried fruit salad and orange juice in a second pan. Bring to the boil, lower the heat, cover and simmer for about 1 hour, until the fruit is tender and no liquid remains. Brush a 1.5 litre / 2½ pint / 6 cup ring mould lightly with oil.

3 Remove the cinnamon stick from the rice. Gently stir in the caster sugar and grated orange rind. Spread out the fruit on the base of the ring tin. Spoon the rice

over, smoothing it down firmly. Cover with clear film and chill for 3–4 hours.

4 Run a knife around the rim of the mould to loosen the rice ring. Invert a serving dish on top and carefully turn both mould and plate over. Serve with a spoonful of whipped cream, if liked.

Rice Condé Sundae

INGREDIENTS

50g/2oz/4 tbsp short grain pudding rice
600ml/1 pint/2½ cups milk
5ml/1 tsp vanilla essence
2.5ml/½ tsp ground cinnamon
45ml/3 tbsp sugar
TO SERVE
raspberries, strawberries or blueberries,
thawed if frozen
chocolate sauce and toasted flaked
almonds (optional)

SERVES 4

123

1 Put the rice, and milk, vanilla essence, cinnamon and sugar into a saucepan. Bring to the boil, stirring constantly, then lower the heat and simmer for 30–40  minutes, stirring occasionally and adding more milk if needed, until the grains are soft.

2 Spoon the mixture into a bowl and set aside to cool, stirring occasionally to prevent a skin from forming. When cold, chill the mixture in the fridge.

3 Just before serving, stir the mixture well. Spoon it into four sundae dishes. Top with raspberries, strawberries or blueberries and add the chocolate sauce and toasted flaked almonds, if using.

COOK'S TIP
Rice puddings are wonderfully versatile.
Try this with dates or apricots stewed in a syrup
flavoured with rosewater. For a very rich pudding,
use half milk and half cream; for slimmers, use
semi-skimmed milk and top with fresh fruit
and natural yogurt.

Thai Rice Cake

INGREDIENTS

*225g / 8oz / generous 1 cup Thai fragrant rice
or jasmine rice
1 litre / 1¾ pints / 4 cups milk
115g / 4oz / ½ cup caster sugar
6 cardamom pods, cracked open
2 bay leaves
300ml / ½ pint / 1¼ cups whipping cream
6 eggs, separated*
TOPPING
*300ml / ½ pint / 1¼ cups double cream
200g / 7oz / scant 1 cup low-fat cream cheese,
softened
5ml / 1 tsp vanilla essence
grated rind of 1 lemon
40g / 1½oz / 3 tbsp caster sugar
soft berry fruits and sliced star fruit and kiwi
fruit, to decorate*

SERVES 8–10

124

1 Grease and base line a deep 25cm/10in round cake tin. Bring a large saucepan of unsalted water to the boil and cook the rice for 3 minutes. Drain the rice thoroughly.

2 Return the rice to the pan. Add the milk, sugar, cracked cardamoms and bay leaves. Bring to the boil, then lower the heat and simmer for 20 minutes, stirring occasionally. Tip the mixture into a bowl and set it aside to cool.

3 Remove the bay leaves and cardamom husks from the mixture. Beat in the whipping cream, then the egg yolks. Preheat the oven to 180°C/350°F/Gas 4.

4 Whisk the egg whites in a clean, dry bowl until soft peaks form. Fold into the rice mixture. Spoon into the prepared tin and bake for 45–50 minutes, until risen and golden brown. The centre should be slightly wobbly – it will firm up as it cools.

5 Chill the cooked rice cake overnight in the tin, then turn out on a large serving plate. Whip the double cream until stiff, then mix with the cream cheese, vanilla essence, lemon rind and sugar.

6 Cover the top and sides of the cake with the cream mixture, swirling it attractively. Decorate with the soft berry fruits and the sliced star fruit and kiwi fruit.

Mangoes with Sticky Rice

INGREDIENTS

115g / 4oz / generous ½ cup white glutinous
(sticky) rice
175ml / 6fl oz / ¾ cup thick coconut milk
45ml / 3 tbsp sugar
pinch of salt
2 ripe mangoes
strips of pared lime rind, to decorate

SERVES 4

1 Rinse the glutinous rice thoroughly in several changes of cold water. Leave to soak overnight in a bowl of fresh, cold water.

2 Drain the rice and spread it in an even layer in a steamer lined with muslin or cheese-cloth. Cover and steam for about 20 minutes, or until the grains are tender.

3 Meanwhile, skim off 45ml/3 tbsp from the top of the coconut milk and set it aside. Heat the remaining coconut milk with the sugar and salt in a saucepan. Stir until the sugar dissolves, then bring to the boil. Pour into a bowl and cool slightly.

4 Tip the rice into a bowl and pour over the sweetened coconut milk. Stir well, leave to stand for 10–15 minutes so that the rice absorbs some of the liquid, then spoon into a serving dish.

5 Peel the mangoes and slice the flesh thinly. Arrange the fruit on top of the rice pudding and drizzle over the reserved coconut milk. Decorate the pudding with strips of lime rind.

Index